MasterCook
USER'S MANUAL

MasterCook 3.0

Windows Program by Alexander Perelberg and David Lee
Macintosh Program by Steve Pederson and Rick Matejka
The MasterCook 3.0 Design and Development Team: Don Bayless, Debbie Lynn, David Macdonald, Jeff Mayzurk, Matt Montgomery, Tarica Spilman, Charles Walker

IT IS ILLEGAL TO MAKE UNAUTHORIZED COPIES OF THIS SOFTWARE

LIMITATIONS ON WARRANTY

Contents

Contents

Contents

Contents

1

WELCOME

Chapter 1

Welcome

Regardless of whether you've purchased MasterCook, MasterCook Deluxe, or the Cooking Light Digital Cookbook — no matter whether your computer is a PC running Windows or an Apple Macintosh… welcome to MasterCook 3.0 — the most sophisticated and powerful cooking program ever written. MasterCook lets you organize and manage all your recipes, makes it easy to make sure you're eating healthy meals, and makes shopping easier than ever.

About this Manual

This manual covers the entire MasterCook 3.0 family of products, including MasterCook (for Windows 3.1, and Windows 95), MasterCook for Macintosh, MasterCook Deluxe, and the MasterCook Cooking Light Digital Cookbook. All these products work in the same way, although in some cases the methods you use to accomplish certain tasks may be different on a PC than they are on a Macintosh. When this occurs, it is clearly noted; please be sure to follow the instructions carefully.

Some of the Things MasterCook Can Do for You

MasterCook makes cooking more enjoyable because it automates your recipe filing and meal planning. Just look at some of the many ways MasterCook can save you time and help you enjoy cooking more:

- **Never lose track of recipes.** How many times have you clipped a recipe out of the newspaper or written one down on a scrap of paper — only to be unable to find it when you needed it? With MasterCook, your recipes are always at your fingertips.
- **Save time finding the right recipe for the occasion — instantly.** Just tell MasterCook what ingredients you have on hand or the foods you'd like to eat and it will find appropriate recipes in a fraction of the time it would take you to consult a single cookbook.
- **E-mail your recipes to friends on the Internet.** With MasterCook, a modem, and Internet access, you can send your recipes to friends and family down the street — or around the world — all with the click of a mouse button. You can also download and import many of the tens of thousands of recipes available from Internet newsgroups and web sites (including the MasterCook web site), as well as from America Online™, CompuServe™, Prodigy™, and the Microsoft Network™, among others.
- **Print your recipes the way *you* want.** Print your recipes with any typeface you want — and on a variety of page sizes, including 3 x 5 and 4 x 6 recipe cards and half-page booklets. With MasterCook it's easier than ever to make your recipes look great.
- **Print complete shopping lists automatically.** Just tell MasterCook which recipes you plan to prepare and it will create a complete shopping list of the ingredients you need to purchase, including the amount of each ingredient. You can even sort your shopping list by store location, to make shopping more efficient.
- **Create quick nutritional analyses of foods, recipes, and even entire meals.** MasterCook uses nutritional data from the United States Department of Agriculture and other respected sources to provide quick, convenient nutritional analyses of the foods you enjoy.

- **Get quick access to information about cooking and foods.** MasterCook features built-in "hypertext"-like links to all sorts of information on food and cooking techniques. Depending on the version of MasterCook you've purchased, these resources can include a graphical utensils library, video tips for food preparation, a built-in cooking glossary, a table of yields and equivalents, and suggestions for seasonings and food substitutions.

Calling Sierra's Technical Support

Contact Technical Support if you have any problem with the installation of MasterCook or if you experience difficulties with the program due to incompatibility or Windows error messages. Please note: Before contacting Sierra Technical Support about printing problems, contact your printer manufacturer for the latest drivers.

Sierra On-Line Technical Support provides assistance through a number of venues. Please use a modem or fax machine, if you have access to one; they are often the best way to solve a problem.

Sierra Technical Support

Voice Automated Line:	206-644-4343
Fax Line:	206-644-7697

Sierra Technical Support e-mail

Sierra's BBS:	206-644-0112
America On Line:	Keyword: Sierra
CompuServe:	Go sierra
Sierra Internet Website:	http://www.sierra.com
Internet Mail:	support@sierra.com

Sierra Direct Sales Group

Our Direct Sales personnel are here to help you with problems concerning disk or documentation replacement, upgrades, or buying any other Sierra products.

Voice phone:	800-757-7707
Fax phone:	408-644-2018
Sierra Direct Mail:	Sierra Direct
	P.O. Box 3404
	Salinas, CA 93912

Sierra European Technical Support

In Europe, please contact our office in England. The Customer Service number is (44) 1734-304227 and the fax number is (44) 1734-303201.

Chapter 1

Sierra On-Line Limited
4 Brewery Court
The Old Brewery
Theale, Reading, Berkshire
RG7 5AJ UNITED KINGDOM

Disk or Documentation Replacement

Sierra will replace defective disks and documentation for the first 90 days of ownership free of charge. After 90 days all requests are subject to shipping and handling fees.

- Disk replacement: All requests within the warranty period must include a copy of your sales receipt and disk #1. Include a note telling us why you need disk replacement and where to send them. If you are outside the 90-day warranty period, please include $10 to cover shipping and handling.

- Document replacement: Requests within the warranty period must include: a copy of your sales receipt, a photocopy of disk #1 (please do not send the disk), a note telling us why documentation is being replaced, and a shipping address. Requests past the 90-day warranty period, please include $5 to cover shipping and handling.

Send all requests for refunds, exchanges and disk or documentation replacement to:
Sierra On-Line Fulfillment
P.O. Box 485
Coarsegold, CA 93614

If you decide to write or fax, please fill out the attached Technical Support Request form and return it to Sierra Technical Support. This will give us the information we need to help you as efficiently as possible.

MasterCook Web Site and Cooking Forum BBS

In addition to our free telephone technical support, you can also receive technical support on Sierra On-Line's MasterCook site on the Internet's World Wide Web and on our 28.8 k-baud BBS, the MasterCook Cooking Forum. In addition to technical support, the MasterCook section of the Sierra web site offers recipes that you can download for free, cooking tips from culinary experts, advice and recipes from the featured Chef of the Month, and many links to other food and recipe sites. The MasterCook web page address is **http://www.mastercook.com.**

For those without Internet access, Sierra runs the MasterCook BBS, where you can also receive free technical support, leave messages for other MasterCook customers, and choose from over 20,000 recipes to download. The Sierra Cooking Forum BBS number is **(512) 327-9814**. Before you call, please set your communication software's terminal settings to VT-100 emulation, 8 bits, 1 stop bit, no parity, and full duplex.

About MasterCook's Nutrition Features

The Ingredients List MasterCook uses to calculate the nutritional content of recipes and menus is a database of over 5,500 food items prepared using United States Department of Agriculture (USDA) publications. Additional information was obtained from food manufacturers. To make this list easier and more practical for cooks to use in creating recipes, we have in some instances shortened the names of foods, but always with the intent of retaining the USDA's meaning as to the specific nature of the food. More information about USDA nutritional publications can be obtained by writing:

> Superintendent of Documents
> U.S. Government Printing Office
> Washington, D.C. 20402

Or, if you have questions about the Ingredients List, you can call our technical support line and we'll be happy to help you.

A Disclaimer

We are not medical doctors and we are not registered dieticians. Therefore, neither the MasterCook program nor the user manual can or will make recommendations about what you should or should not eat. MasterCook is designed to calculate the nutritional values of foods *that you choose to eat* based upon the most recent available data from the United States Department of Agriculture.

The nutrient values in foods may vary substantially, depending upon such variables as geography, soil content, season, ripeness, processing, genetics, and method of preparation. The values in the MasterCook Ingredients List are meant to be typical but may not in all instances accurately reflect the nutritional content of the food you actually consume. Moreover, in some instances a nutrient value for a given foodstuff may be undetermined; in these cases, the letters "N/A" are used to indicate that the information was not available.

When MasterCook calculates the nutritional values of your recipes, it attempts to offer a means of taking into account the method by which the food is to be prepared. For example, there are in the Ingredients List different listings for some foods depending on whether they are cooked or raw. When determining the nutrient values for a recipe, however, the component nutrients are summed, so changes in the nutrient values of foods due to preparation are not always taken into account. For example, if cooking wine is used in the preparation of a recipe, the total nutritional value of the cooking wine is added to the nutritional value of the recipe, without consideration of the effect of the evaporation of the wine's alcohol. As you become experienced in using MasterCook, you will be better able to determine when to include such values in your recipes.

For these reasons, please use the MasterCook nutritional profiles as approximate guides to the nutrient content of your recipes. Those persons on special diets for the treatment of disease may require more specific nutrient data and should consult their personal physicians, registered dieticians, and/or food manufacturers.

Chapter 1

Where to Go Next

Now that you've read all about MasterCook, it's time to install it and use it. The next chapter, "Getting Started," will help you install MasterCook on your system and will give you a brief "guided tour" of MasterCook. From there, you will probably want to experiment. We suggest opening one of the cookbooks that come with MasterCook and then try opening, searching for, and printing recipes. This will give you some idea of the ways MasterCook can help you organize your cooking and shopping.

2

GETTING STARTED

Chapter 2

Getting Started

This chapter covers everything you need to know to install and begin using MasterCook. First, there is a brief inventory of what you'll need in order to successfully run MasterCook on your computer system. Next, step-by-step instructions show you how to install MasterCook.

Once you've installed MasterCook, follow the instructions for starting the program, and then read about the MasterCook environment. Instructions are provided to allow you to configure the program to your liking, letting you specify the way you want MasterCook to help you type and save your recipes. Finally, a conceptual overview of MasterCook is provided to help you understand how the program has been designed to imitate the way you already store and look up recipes.

Installing the MasterCook Program and Cookbooks

The Setup program on your MasterCook disk makes installing MasterCook and its cookbook files quick and easy. When you run the Setup program, it asks you to specify the hard drive on which you'd like to install MasterCook. It then creates a directory or folder (titled / MSTRCOOK on Windows and "MasterCook" on Macintosh) on your hard drive. This directory contains the MasterCook program and cookbook files.

MasterCook comes on 3.5-inch floppy disks; MasterCook Deluxe and the MasterCook-Cooking Light Digital Cookbook come on CD-ROM disks. When you run the MasterCook Setup program, it decompresses the MasterCook program and cookbook files and copies them to the hard drive you specify. Those products that come on CD-ROM use graphics and video files that are extremely large and thus are not copied to your hard drive. If you're running Windows 95, you can also run MasterCook directly from the CD-ROM disk without installing the program at all.

Installing MasterCook

Before installing MasterCook on a PC or Macintosh, please make sure that your computer meets the following system requirements:

For a PC system:

- Microsoft Windows 3.1 or later
- MS-DOS version 5.0 or higher
- 386, 486, Pentium or higher IBM or compatible PC
- At least 3 MB of RAM
- At least 3 MB free on your hard disk

  and if you're installing MasterCook Deluxe or the Cooking Light Digital Cookbook:
- CD-ROM drive

For a Macintosh system:

- A Macintosh Plus running System 6.0 or later
- At least 3 MB of RAM
- At least 3 MB free on your hard disk
  and if you're installing MasterCook Deluxe or the Cooking Light Digital Cookbook:
- CD-ROM drive

To install MasterCook from floppy disks (PC only):

1. Put the MasterCook Disk 1 in your 3 1/2-inch disk drive.

2. Choose Run from the File menu (on Windows 3.1 and 3.11) or from the Start Button (Windows 95).

3. Type N:SETUP, where N is the letter of your 3 1/2-inch disk drive, and click the OK button.

4. Follow the on-screen instructions to install the program.

To install MasterCook from floppy disks (Macintosh only):

1. Put the MasterCook Disk 1 in your 3 1/2-inch disk drive.

    A window appears containing a single icon, titled "MasterCook Setup."

2. Double-click the MasterCook Setup program icon.

    The MasterCook Setup program starts, displaying a dialog box that lets you choose the hard disk on which to install MasterCook.

3. If you have more than one hard disk (or other mass storage device) on your system, specify the hard disk on which you'd like to install MasterCook.

4. Click the Install button.

5. Follow the on-screen instructions to install the program.

To install MasterCook from CD-ROM (PC only):

1. Put the MasterCook CD in your CD-ROM drive.

2. Choose Run from the File menu (on Windows 3.1 and 3.11) or from the Start Button (Windows 95).

3. Type N:SETUP, where N is the letter of your CD drive and click the OK button.

4. Follow the on-screen instructions to install the program.

D: \ PC TOOLS \ SYSTEM \ SIERRA

To install MasterCook from CD-ROM (Macintosh only):

1. Put the MasterCook CD in your CD-ROM drive.

    A window appears containing a single icon, titled "MasterCook Setup program."

2. Double-click the MasterCook Setup program icon.

3. If you have more than one hard disk (or other mass storage device) on your system, specify the hard disk on which you'd like to install MasterCook.

4. Click the Install button.

5. Follow the on-screen instructions to install the program.

Starting MasterCook

When you install MasterCook on your computer, the Setup program automatically creates a folder and icons for the MasterCook program and for each of the cookbooks that come with MasterCook. You can start MasterCook by double-clicking its program icon or any one of its cookbook icons.

To start MasterCook:

■   Double-click the MasterCook program icon or any of the cookbook icons.

    For example, if you wish to open the Cooking Light Digital Cookbook, double-click the Cooking Light cookbook icon.

    The MasterCook program starts up, displaying the MasterCook splash screen, followed by a dialog box telling you that MasterCook is reading the Ingredients List. The Open Cookbook dialog box appears, containing a list of cookbooks in the MasterCook directory (folder).

Opening a Cookbook

Once you've started the MasterCook application, the Open Cookbook dialog box appears in the center of the screen, to allow you to choose a cookbook to open.

This dialog box appears every time you start the MasterCook application (unless you start MasterCook by double-clicking a cookbook icon). To open an existing cookbook, select it from the Cookbooks list in the Open Cookbook dialog box and then click the Open button. Otherwise, you can click the New button to create a new cookbook. (For information on creating new cookbooks, see "Creating a New Cookbook" in Chapter Three, "Cookbooks.")

To Open a Cookbook:

■   Click the cookbook icon and then click the OK button — or double-click the cookbook icon.

The cookbook is opened and appears in its own window.

The MasterCook Environment

When you start MasterCook and open a cookbook, you're working in the MasterCook application program environment. In addition to the menu bar and cookbook window, the MasterCook environment contains a variety of other types of windows that let you perform different tasks. For example, recipes, shopping lists, menus, and meal plans all have their own types of windows, because you do different things with them. These windows can be placed on top of one another, and you can move from window to window with a mouse-button click.

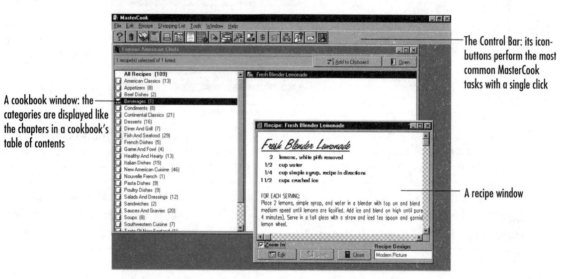

The Control Bar: its icon-buttons perform the most common MasterCook tasks with a single click

A cookbook window: the categories are displayed like the chapters in a cookbook's table of contents

A recipe window

At the top of the MasterCook screen is the menu bar, from which you choose the commands that you want MasterCook to execute.

The Control Bar

Beneath the menu bar is the Control Bar, a strip of *icon-buttons* (buttons containing symbolic pictures rather than words) that let you perform the most common MasterCook functions — for example, printing, exporting, deleting, and mailing recipes — with a single button click.

When you move the arrow pointer over an icon-button, MasterCook automatically tells you which task the it performs by displaying a text message describing its function on the right side of the Control Bar. For a complete description of the Control Bar and its functions, see "The Control Bar," in Chapter Seven, "Tools."

Chapter 2

Cookbook Windows

When you open cookbook files, their windows appear below the Control Bar. Each cookbook window contains the name of the cookbook in its title bar. The names of the cookbook's categories are displayed in a List View format on the left side of the cookbook window like the chapter titles in a cookbook's table of contents.

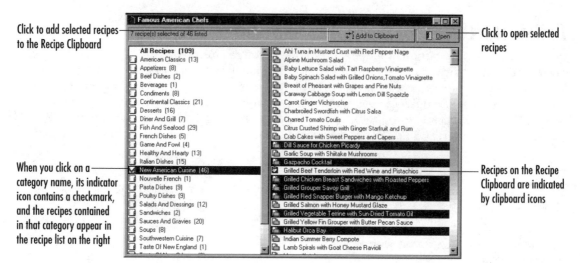

Click to add selected recipes to the Recipe Clipboard

Click to open selected recipes

When you click on a category name, its indicator icon contains a checkmark, and the recipes contained in that category appear in the recipe list on the right

Recipes on the Recipe Clipboard are indicated by clipboard icons

To the left of each category name is an *indicator icon*; when the cookbook contains recipes for a category, a number in parentheses (representing the number of recipes in the cookbook for that category) appears to the immediate right of the category name.

▶ **NOTE:** Because the Macintosh version of MasterCook includes different cookbook views, you can open a MasterCook for Macintosh cookbook in a view other than the List View shown above. For more information on cookbook views, see Chapter 3, "Cookbooks."

When you click on a category name, that category's recipes appear in a list of recipes on the right side of the cookbook window and a checkmark appears in the category's indicator icon. To open recipes from the cookbook, click on the names of the categories in the cookbook that contain the recipes that you wish to open. (Click on "All Recipes" at the top of the list of categories to display all recipes in the cookbook.) Select a contiguous group of categories (category names adjacent to one another in the list) by holding down the SHIFT key as you click on the first and last categories in the group that you wish to select. As each new category is selected, its recipes are added to the list of recipes on the right. To make a noncontiguous selection (categories are not adjacent), hold down the CTRL (Control) key as you click each category (on a Macintosh, hold down the COMMAND or "Apple" key next to the SPACEBAR).

Next, choose the recipes that you want to open from the recipes list on the right. Again, to choose a contiguous group of recipes, hold down the SHIFT key as you click on the first and last recipes in the group; press the CTRL key (the COMMAND key on a Macintosh) and click on recipe names to choose a noncontiguous group. When you've selected the recipes you want to display, click the Open button. The selected recipes are opened.

The Recipe Clipboard

MasterCook maintains a permanent Recipe Clipboard, which lets you group together recipes from one or more cookbooks. You can add recipes to the Recipe Clipboard — and remove recipes from it — one at a time or in groups. Use the Recipe Clipboard when you want to combine recipes from different cookbooks into a new cookbook or when you want a temporary storage place for recipes that you may want to browse.

Recipes are placed on the Recipe Clipboard in several different ways. You can click on the names of recipes in the cookbook window and then click the Add to Clipboard button; you can drag recipes from a cookbook onto the Recipe Clipboard; or you can use the Search Recipes command on the Recipe menu to find recipes that match certain criteria; the recipes that MasterCook finds are placed on the Recipe Clipboard.

Click to remove recipes from the Recipe Clipboard

To make a contiguous selection, hold down the SHIFT key as you click on recipe names; for a non-contiguous selection, hold down the CTRL key as you click them

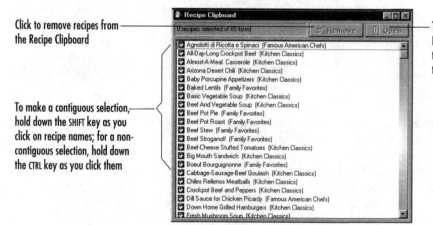

To view and edit recipes on the Recipe Clipboard, click on the recipes that you want to open, and then click the Open button

When you perform a recipe search, the Recipe Clipboard window is automatically opened and the recipes you located are displayed. You can choose groups of recipes to display from the Recipe Clipboard window, just as you do from the cookbook window. After a search, the window remains open to allow you to continue to open recipes from your last search. To display the Recipe Clipboard, choose Recipe Clipboard from the Window menu.

Chapter 2

Customizing the MasterCook Environment with Preferences

Everybody has different tastes, especially in the kitchen, so we've made it easy for you to personalize your MasterCook environment with the Preferences command on the Tools menu. You may want to experiment with the different settings on the Preferences dialog box to find which options work best for you.

Among the other things you can do to customize your MasterCook environment are:
- Specify which measurement system to use — American, Metric, or Combined.
- Choose whether to use fractions or decimal numbers for amounts in recipes.
- Specify whether or not to display the MasterCook Ingredients List in Recipes.
- Specify if you want to use abbreviations for unit measures (tbsp for tablespoon, tsp for teaspoon, etc.).
- Choose whether or not to save the search criteria used in your last recipe search the next time you use the Search Recipes command.
- Choose whether to use the name of the last recipe author saved to disk as the author of new recipes.

The Window Menu

MasterCook uses the Window menu to help you keep track of windows in the MasterCook environment. In addition to displaying the names of all open windows, this menu contains commands for manipulating windows in MasterCook: Close All, Close All Recipes, Hide/ Show Control Bar, Recipe Clipboard, and Import Results. Close All closes all open windows, and Close All Recipes closes all recipe windows but leaves cookbook windows open. Hide/ Show Control Bar lets you choose whether to display the Control Bar.

Choosing "Recipe Clipboard" from the Window menu makes the Recipe Clipboard the current active window. Import Results lists the names of recipes in which possible translation errors may have occurred when importing recipes into MasterCook with the Import Recipes command or when opening a non-MasterCook recipe file (such as a text file exported from MasterCook or another recipe program) with the Open command. Import Results also lists the names or recipes with the same names as recipes already in the cookbook into which you're importing. MasterCook appends onto the end of each duplicate file name a number that reflects the order in which the recipe was introduced into the cookbook. So, for example, if you already had a recipe for "Brownies" in the cookbook and tried to import recipes also named "Brownies" from two different cookbooks, MasterCook would rename them "Brownies2" and "Brownies3".

The bottom portion of the Window menu lists all open MasterCook windows. Cookbooks are listed by name; recipes, menus, meal plans, and shopping lists are preceded by a label ("Recipe:", "Menu:", etc.) identifying the type of window.

The Help Menu

Whenever you need assistance using MasterCook, use MasterCook's online help. For Windows users, this is to be found on the Help menu. The Index command displays a list of online help topics; clicking on a topic in this list displays information on the topic. The Basics command provides background information and assistance in getting started using MasterCook. The Keyboard command describes keyboard shortcuts and tips; Commands offers detailed explanations of all commands found on MasterCook menus. Finally, Using Help provides information on using the online help system.

For Macintosh users, MasterCook provides two types of online assistance, both of which are found on the Macintosh Guide menu (next to the Application menu on the far right side of the menu bar): the MasterCook Online Help program and Balloon Help. The MasterCook Online Help program offers assistance in four areas: program basics, keyboard shortcuts, MasterCook commands, and information on using the Help program; the Index lets you choose which of these areas to review, and also lets you search for information on specific aspects of the program. To use the Online Help program, choose Help from the Guide menu.

Balloon Help helps you learn about using MasterCook by displaying information in "balloons" that appear when you move the mouse pointer over different items on the MasterCook screen. For example, moving the pointer over a cookbook window displays different information on how the different parts of the cookbook window work. To use Balloon Help, choose Show Balloons from the Guide menu.

Quitting MasterCook

When you wish to end a session of using MasterCook, choose the Exit command from the File menu (or the Quit command on the File menu, if you're using a Macintosh).

To quit the MasterCook program:

■   Choose Exit from the File menu (on a Macintosh, choose Quit from the File menu).

   The MasterCook application program quits, returning you to the Windows or Macintosh desktop.

The following section provides a conceptual overview of MasterCook, to give you an outline of how the program works before you proceed to use the program to create your own cookbooks, recipes, and shopping lists.

Chapter 2

An Overview of MasterCook

MasterCook is designed to let you create, file, and retrieve recipes the same way that you do now, only in a more efficient and enjoyable manner. So before we discuss how MasterCook works, perhaps we should review how you probably file and retrieve recipes now.

Recipes, Cookbooks, and Ingredients

When you want to prepare a meal from a recipe, you probably refer to a cookbook or to your own file of recipes. If you know the recipe you want, you try to locate its name in the index of the appropriate cookbook or look for it under the appropriate index tab of your card file. If your search is successful, you then turn to the page of the cookbook or pull out the index card — and there's your recipe.

MasterCook works the same way. Recipes are stored in files on disk called, appropriately enough, *cookbooks*. To look for and display recipes with MasterCook, you first open a cook-book — just as you look for recipes in real life by opening a physical cookbook. MasterCook lets you create as many cookbooks as you have disk space for, and the recipes in each cook-book can be organized according to whatever categories you choose. You can give a cookbook any name you like, provided it is a legal Windows or Macintosh file name.

When you create a new MasterCook recipe or retrieve an existing one, it appears in its own window. You can open as many recipes at one time as you have system memory for, and "flip through" recipe windows as you would through the pages of a cookbook.

Just as cookbooks are made up of recipes, recipes are made up of ingredients. MasterCook makes it easy to create recipes because it already comes with an Ingredients List database of over 5,500 of the most commonly used recipe ingredients, so you'll rarely have to type a full ingredient name! And because each ingredient has a full nutritional profile and store location accompanying it, you can automatically create nutritional analyses and shopping lists of your recipes — with just the click of a button. In addition, you can add thousands of your own ingredients to the MasterCook Ingredients List, if you wish.

How MasterCook's Nutritional Analysis Works

MasterCook puts a wealth of nutritional information at your fingertips. With MasterCook, you can prepare a nutritional analysis of a recipe or look up the nutritional content of individual foods automatically, without scanning nutrition tables or doing a lot of complicated nutritional calculations.

To provide this instant nutritional analysis, MasterCook comes with an Ingredients List that includes nutrient values for over 5,500 food items. The nutrition information for this Ingredients List comes primarily from United States Department of Agriculture (USDA) research publications (as well as other sources). For its nutritional research, the USDA attempted to use standard (if not always average) quantities in common household measurement units of the most commonly eaten foods prepared in the most typical manner. For this reason, many of their descriptions of foods can be both encoded with abbreviations and at the same time very lengthy, often too lengthy for the average consumer to use in a recipe. We have condensed the USDA food descriptions into usable food item names in average quantities, so that they're easy to use in your recipes and menus.

Sometimes an item on the Ingredients List describes a foodstuff for which the nutritional information is based on a whole unit, such as an egg, a banana, a fillet of fish, etc. — as opposed to a standard measurement unit, such as a cup, a tablespoon, etc. So, for example, if you were to specify a cup of bananas, but had chosen the item in the Ingredients List for whole rather than sliced bananas, your nutrition information for the recipe would be slightly inaccurate (a cup of sliced bananas contains about 1 ¼ whole bananas).

MasterCook helps you avoid this problem by:
* Making the food item name as descriptive of the item as possible
* Displaying in **bold type** the names of all items with nutritional data based on whole units

So, for example, in the Ingredients List the nutritional data for the item "sliced bananas" is based on one cup of sliced bananas, whereas the nutritional information for the item "**bananas**" is based on one whole banana.

> ▶ **NOTE:** All food items in the Ingredients List have weight amounts included with their nutritional data, so any ingredient entered in a recipe using a weight-based measurement unit (ounces, pounds, grams, etc.) should provide an accurate nutritional profile.

It's important to note that you don't have to use MasterCook's Ingredients List to specify recipe ingredients. MasterCook allows you to type any ingredient you want in a recipe. If you want, you can even tell MasterCook *not* to display the Ingredients List when you're creating recipes (see "Setting MasterCook Preferences," in Chapter Eight, "Tools"). If MasterCook can't find the name of an ingredient in its food list, however, it can't provide you with nutritional information on that ingredient.

This doesn't mean that you have to use the standard food list names for ingredients if you want to get nutritional profiles of your recipes. In addition to using the food list names (in which case you can access the MasterCook nutritional information) or your own ingredient names (in which case you can't), there is a third way of entering ingredients that combines the two approaches. This third approach is called *creating a link* between an ingredient name and nutritional information for a food item in the list. This technique lets you type the ingredients for a recipe in any manner that you want, then link the ingredient names to nutritional information already maintained by MasterCook. For more information on creating links, see "Recipe Ingredients and Nutritional Information" in Chapter Four, "Recipes."

Chapter 2

Daily Values

MasterCook includes the FDA-USDA Daily Values, the basis for all food product nutritional information labeling in the United States.

These Daily Values provide nutritional guidelines for the average consumer, telling you how much (in percentages) of a day's worth of fat, cholesterol, sodium, carbohydrate, protein, and selected vitamins and minerals are provided by a serving of the packaged goods. The Daily Values use two different tables, one for a 2,000 calorie diet (applicable to women, children, and men over 50) and one for a 2,500 calorie diet (representing the needs of younger men, teenage boys, and all very active people).

With MasterCook, you can now create a recipe and see what percentage of your daily needs it meets, both for 2,000 and 2,500 calorie diets. Use these values with moderation, however; a food doesn't need to have 50 to 100 percent of a Daily Value to be high in that nutrient. A good rule of thumb: if a recipe has 20 percent or more of the Daily Value, it may be considered high in that nutrient. Persons on restricted diets should be especially careful when using Daily Values as guidelines and should do so under the guidance of a physician.

The Daily Values dialog box provides nutritional information for your recipes using the FDA-USDA food product label format

Daily Values			
Amount Per Serving:	Calories: 2137	Calories from Fat:	923
		% Daily Value* 2000 Calorie Diet	% Daily Value* 2500 Calorie Diet
Total Fat: 102.6g		158%	128%
Saturated Fat:	20.5g	103%	82%
Cholesterol: 85.4mg		28%	28%
Sodium: 884.5mg		37%	37%
Total Carbohydrate:	239.7g	80%	64%
Dietary Fiber:	9.8g	39%	33%
Protein: 63.8g		128%	102%
Vitamin A: 30%	Vitamin C: 62%	Calcium: 21%	Iron: 92%

* Your Daily Values may vary higher or lower depending on your calorie needs.

Close

Where to Go Next

Now that you have a basic understanding of how MasterCook works, you're ready to begin using the program. You may want to start by reading about cookbooks in Chapter Three, and try opening one of the cookbooks that came with the program. Next, you might want to try creating your own recipes using the instructions in Chapter Four, "Recipes," then try creating a shopping list for a recipe or printing a recipe. If you have any questions as you work, refer to the online Help program. Before you know it, you'll be managing all your favorite recipes with MasterCook.

3

COOKBOOKS

Chapter 3

About Cookbooks

Anyone who has done much cooking knows that cookbooks are structured collections of recipes, arranged to make finding and using recipes as convenient as possible. For this reason, cookbooks are usually organized into chapters based upon some sort of categorization of recipes. For example, recipes may be categorized by:

- the type of food — poultry, beef dishes, vegetarian meals, etc.
- course or position in the meal — appetizers, salads, main dishes, desserts, etc.
- regional, national, or ethnic foods — Chinese, Italian, Cajun, Provençal, etc.
- the author or source of the recipe

Almost all conventional cookbooks are organized by categories, but usually by only one type of category — with each recipe in the cookbook assigned to only one category. MasterCook's electronic cookbooks are organized by categories as well. Unlike conventional cookbooks, however, MasterCook cookbooks can be organized any way you like — by the type of food, by course, by region or ethnic origin, by source — all at the same time! This is because Master-Cook lets you create whichever categories you like and assign multiple categories to a single recipe. So, for example, a single recipe can be an appetizer, a Tex-Mex favorite, a cheese dish, and the December 1995 Recipe of the Month from your favorite cooking magazine.

And what exactly are MasterCook's "electronic cookbooks"? MasterCook cookbooks are the *files* MasterCook uses to store your recipes. All computer programs use files to let you save your work once your computer's power is turned off — word processor files are usually called *documents*, spreadsheet program files are called *worksheets*, etc. These files reside on your hard drive or on a floppy disk and can be copied to different directories and disks, so you can make backups of them and give copies to others who own and use the same program.

MasterCook's cookbook files can be given any name you like. On Windows, cookbook file names can be as long as 80 characters (on both Windows 3.1 and Windows 95; MasterCook has supported long file names for cookbooks since Windows 3.0). On the Macintosh version of MasterCook, file names can be as long as 31 characters. Each cookbook can contain up to 8,000 recipes, but there's no need to keep all of your recipes in one cookbook unless you prefer to work that way. You could, for instance, have one cookbook devoted entirely to low-fat recipes, another for desserts, and so on. However you decide to organize your recipes, Master-Cook makes it easy to manage them.

This chapter provides instructions for working with cookbooks — opening and closing them; creating new cookbooks; renaming and backing up cookbooks; deleting cookbooks, and importing, exporting, and copying recipes. Also covered are the different ways to view your cookbooks and how to create custom cookbook designs.

Creating a New Cookbook

To create a new cookbook:

1. Choose New Cookbook from the File menu.

   The New Cookbook dialog box appears.

Type the cookbook name here

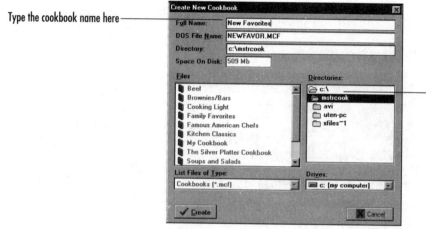

Choose the directory (folder) and/or disk-drive where you want to save the cookbook file

2. Type a name for the new cookbook.

3. Click the Create button.

   The cookbook window for the new cookbook appears on the screen. The Categories dialog box also appears. You'll create the categories for the new cookbook using this dialog box.

Type the name for each category you wish to create here...

...then click the Add button to add the category to the list

Click the Use Template button to use the existing template categories

4. For each category that you wish to add to the cookbook, type the category name and then click the Add button.

   As you add each category, it appears in alphabetical order in the list box.

Chapter 3

5. Click the OK button when you've finished adding categories.

    The cookbook window displays your new categories.

Opening a Cookbook

To open a cookbook:

1. Choose Open Cookbook from the File menu or click the Open icon-button on the Control Bar.

    The Open Cookbook dialog box appears.

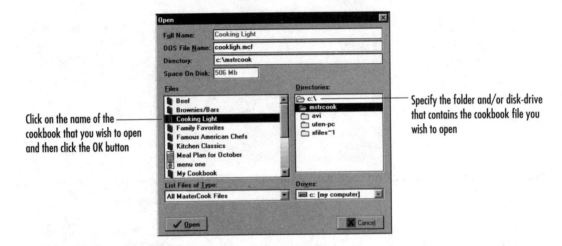

Click on the name of the cookbook that you wish to open and then click the OK button

Specify the folder and/or disk-drive that contains the cookbook file you wish to open

2. Click the file name for the cookbook you wish to open and click Open, or double-click the cookbook file name.

    The cookbook is opened and its cookbook window appears.

The Cookbook Window

When you open a cookbook, the cookbook's window appears. The cookbook window is a software version of a cookbook's table of contents: on the left are the cookbook's categories, laid out like the chapters of a cookbook; on the right are the recipes in the selected category or categories. You can use this aspect of the cookbook window to find recipes by category or type, just as you would use a table of contents in a standard cookbook. You can also use the cookbook window for copying and deleting recipes; creating shopping lists, menus, and meal plans; sending recipes via electronic mail; and much more. The cookbook window is a key part of MasterCook's "electronic cookbook," as it provides quick and easy access to the recipes contained within.

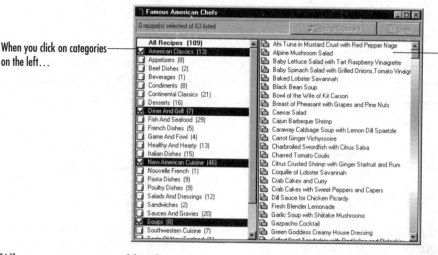

When you click on categories on the left...

... recipes in those categories appear on the right

When you open a cookbook, you see a list of categories on the left side of the window; a number next to each category name indicates the number of recipes in that category. When you click on a category, that category's recipes are added to the recipe list on the right. You can select a contiguous group of categories by holding down the SHIFT key and clicking on the categories that you want; as each new category is selected, its recipes are added to the recipes list on the right. To make a noncontiguous selection, hold down the CONTROL key (COMMAND on a Macintosh) as you click on each recipe name. You can then choose the recipes you want from the recipes list on the right. Again, hold down the SHIFT key and click to choose a contiguous group of recipes; press CONTROL (COMMAND on a Macintosh) and click to choose a noncontiguous group.

Once you've selected a recipe or group of recipes, you can open them by clicking the Open button on the Control Bar. Most of MasterCook's tools also work on selections in the cookbook window — you could, for instance, select a group of recipes and create a shopping list for them by choosing Make Shopping List from the Shopping List menu. And just as you can have more than one cookbook open on your kitchen table, MasterCook doesn't restrict you to using one cookbook at a time. With two or more cookbooks open, you have the flexibility of being able to copy recipes between cookbooks with drag and drop, or to create menus, shopping lists, and nutritional analyses using combined recipes from multiple cookbooks.

The Cookbook Window: Page View (Macintosh only)

MasterCook for Macintosh lets you see cookbooks in different ways: *list view*, which is the "regular" cookbook window described in the previous section; and *page view*, which shows recipes on individual pages, much like they would appear when printed in a book or magazine. MasterCook's page view extends the "electronic cookbook" metaphor by allowing you to flip through pages one at a time, or, if you prefer, to see an index and then jump to a specific page. As an alternative to list view, it's a convenient way to browse a cookbook — to

Chapter 3

look at the pictures, for example, or to read a chef's comments on his or her recipes. And since page view works on the principle of "What You See Is What You Get," you'll see how your recipes will look when printed on paper.

 Note: The Windows version of MasterCook supports Page View in recipe windows, rather than the cookbook window, and while the implementation is different than described here, it offers the same print options (such as recipe cards and half-page booklet printing), although not the same options for browsing and modifying recipe designs.

Page view is actually not one but four different ways of viewing recipes: full page, single-sided; full page, double-sided (front and back); half-page book; and full-page book. Each of the four views (plus the list view) is represented at the top of the cookbook window with an icon-button, so you can switch between different views at any time.

This section covers the basic aspects of the page view: browsing cookbooks and changing the appearance of cookbooks with page layouts and recipe designs. MasterCook also provides powerful editing features for modifying page layouts and creating new designs — please see Appendix A, "Modifying Page Layouts and Recipe Designs," for more information.

To view a cookbook in page view:

1. Open a cookbook as previously described in the "Opening a Cookbook" section of this chapter.

    The cookbook window appears. Because MasterCook saves its settings for each cookbook independently, the cookbook may be opened in either list view *or* page view, depending on which mode you were in the last time you used the cookbook.

2. If necessary, switch to a page view by clicking one of the icon-buttons at the top of the cookbook window.

    The cookbook window changes to reflect the page view you've chosen.

3. Click the forward arrow icon-button or the reverse arrow icon-button to change pages, or type a page number in the page number text box.

    The page you've chosen is displayed in the cookbook window.

▷ **TIP:** You can also use the arrow keys on the keyboard to change pages — the left arrow moves back one page, and the right arrow moves forward one page; holding down the COMMAND key while pressing the left or right arrow keys will move to the first or last page in the cookbook, respectively.

4. Click the Index icon-button to see an index of all recipes in the cookbook.

    The index is displayed with a list of recipe names, and if available, page numbers.

5. Double-click a recipe name to jump to the page containing that recipe in the cookbook.

    The new page is displayed. If necessary, MasterCook reformats all pages in the cookbook up to the current page.

Page Layouts and Recipe Designs

Controlling the way recipes look on the page are *page layouts* and *recipe designs* — MasterCook's "style guides" for displaying cookbooks in page view. Page layouts, as the name implies, control attributes of the physical page: page size, orientation, content areas (number of columns and/or rows), margins, etc. Recipe designs affect the way recipes are formatted on the page: which parts of recipes are displayed and in what order; what fonts are used and their sizes; the alignment of and spacing between various objects; and so on.

MasterCook comes with a variety of page layouts and recipe designs, so it's easy to create attractive cookbook layouts without much effort on your part. What's more, you have the flexibility of being able to combine page layouts and recipe designs any way you want, so you always have control over how cookbooks are displayed and printed.

However, you may want to exercise some caution when experimenting with layouts and recipe designs. For example, MasterCook won't prevent you from using a 24-point font on 3" x 5" index cards, or from trying to use a three-column page layout in half-page book mode, even though these combinations obviously won't work very well. The page layouts and recipe designs included with MasterCook are designed to work well in most situations, though, so you can always revert to the standard settings.

To change the appearance of cookbooks using page layouts and recipe designs:

1. Open a cookbook and switch to page view, if necessary. (See the previous section, "Opening Cookbooks," in this chapter, for more information.)

2. Click on the Page Layout icon-button at the top of the cookbook window and hold down the mouse button.

    A drop-down list appears, containing a list of available page layouts.

3. Choose a page layout from the drop-down list.

    All pages in the cookbook up to the current page are reformatted with the new page layout.

4. Click the Recipe Design icon-button at the top of the cookbook window.

    A drop-down list appears, containing a list of available recipe designs.

5. Choose a recipe design from the drop-down list.

    All pages in the cookbook up to the current page are reformatted with the new recipe design.

Chapter 3

▶ **NOTE:** Reformatting pages can take a long time, especially if the cookbook is large. If you make all of your modifications to the page layout and recipe design on the first page in the cookbook (page one), MasterCook will only reformat that page, which takes almost no time at all. If you hold down the SHIFT key as you make selections from the Layout Tools menus, MasterCook won't reformat until the next time you choose a command from one of the Layout Tools menus, at which time it will reformat the cookbook up to the current page.

The Recipe Clipboard

Some of your favorite cookbooks probably have built-in bookmarks — ribbons that you place across a page to mark recipes for quick reference. MasterCook's equivalent is the Recipe Clipboard, a place where you can put into "temporary storage" those recipes that you may wish to later open or print. The Recipe Clipboard is a convenient place to store recipes when you're trying to combine recipes from several different cookbooks, plan a meal, or create a shopping list. The Recipe Clipboard is always available, even if you don't have a cookbook open — you can display its window at any time by choosing Recipe Clipboard from the Window menu.

There are three ways that you can store recipes on the Recipe Clipboard: click on the recipe names in the cookbook window and then click the Add to Clipboard button; drag recipes from a cookbook onto the Recipe Clipboard window; or use the Search Recipes command to locate recipes that meet the requirements you specify (Search Recipes lets you specify whether you want to replace the recipes on the Recipe Clipboard, add to them, or search only the recipes on the Recipe Clipboard).

 NOTE: Since the Recipe Clipboard may contain recipes from many different cookbooks, recipe names are listed with the cookbook name in parentheses.

Reading MasterCook for Macintosh Cookbooks on a PC

Because both MasterCook for Windows and MasterCook for Macintosh use the same file format, each program can read cookbooks created or edited with the other. You could, for example, create a cookbook file using MasterCook for Windows, edit it on a Macintosh (as explained in the section following this one), and read it again on your PC. If you're using Windows, all you have to do to read a MasterCook for Macintosh cookbook file is:

- Give the cookbook file an "eight and three" file name — an eight-character file name followed by a three-character file extension, with the file extension ".MCF".
- Save the cookbook file on a disk formatted for DOS/Windows.

Reading MasterCook for Windows Cookbooks on a Macintosh

If you have Apple's PC Exchange™ or another DOS mounter installed on your Macintosh, MasterCook can read MasterCook for Windows cookbook files directly from a PC-formatted disk. (PC Exchange ships as part of the MacOS starting with System 7.5; it is available for use with earlier versions of the Macintosh system software as an extension.) For information on reading MasterCook for Windows files with your Macintosh, see Appendix B, "Exchanging Files Between MasterCook for Windows and MasterCook for Macintosh."

Closing a Cookbook

■ Choose Close Cookbook from the File menu or click the cookbook window's close box.

If you've made changes to a recipe or recipes that you haven't yet saved, a dialog box appears for each unsaved recipe, to allow you to save your changes.

Renaming/Copying/Backing Up a Cookbook

You can make a copy of a cookbook, or save a cookbook to a different disk-drive or folder, with the Save Cookbook As command on the File menu. When you save a cookbook with this command, a copy of the cookbook is saved with a new name to the specified folder. The new copy of the cookbook becomes the current open cookbook, and subsequent changes you make to recipes will be saved to the new version of the cookbook. Use this command to rename cookbooks, to back up your cookbook files, or to make copies of your recipes to give to other MasterCook users.

To rename or make a copy of a cookbook:

1. Choose Save Cookbook As from the File menu.

    A dialog box appears with the current name of the cookbook selected.

2. Type a new name for the cookbook and click the Save button.

    A copy of the cookbook is saved with the new cookbook name.

▷ **TIP:** Use the instructions above to back up your cookbooks as you work. First, use Save Cookbook As to save the cookbook to another folder, preferably on another disk, such as a floppy disk you use exclusively for the purpose of making backups. Then use Save Cookbook As again to save the cookbook in its original folder, so that subsequent changes to your recipes and menus will be made to the original version of the cookbook and not to your backup.

Chapter 3

Deleting a Cookbook

The Delete command on the File menu lets you delete one or more cookbooks, so that you don't have to leave MasterCook to remove unwanted cookbook files from your hard disk or floppy disk.

Before you delete a cookbook, you may want to make sure you have a backup copy of it. To make a backup of a cookbook, see "Renaming/Copying/Backing Up a Cookbook," in the preceding section of this chapter.

To delete a cookbook:

1. Choose Delete from the File Menu (Delete Cookbook on a Macintosh).

    The Delete Cookbook dialog box appears, containing a list of cookbooks in the current folder.

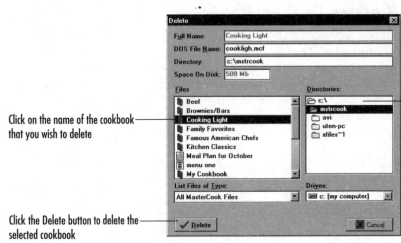

Click on the name of the cookbook that you wish to delete

Specify the folder and/or disk-drive that contains the cookbook to be deleted

Click the Delete button to delete the selected cookbook

2. If the cookbook you wish to delete is in a different folder or on a different disk-drive, open the appropriate folder and/or drive.

3. Click on the file name for the cookbook that you wish to delete.

4. Click the Delete button.

    A dialog box appears, asking you to confirm that you wish to permanently delete the specified cookbook.

5. Click the Delete button to delete the cookbook.

    The cookbook is deleted.

Editing a Cookbook's Categories

Once you've created a cookbook, you can continue to add categories to it, remove categories from it, and rename its categories using the Edit Categories command on the File menu (the Categories on a Macintosh). The Categories command also lets you save the current categories as a *template* to provide instant categories for future cookbooks.

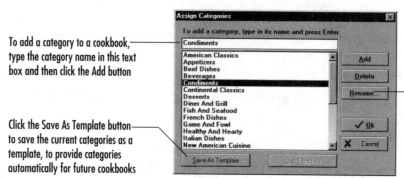

To add a category to a cookbook, type the category name in this text box and then click the Add button

To rename or delete a category, click on its name in this list and then click the Rename or Delete button

Click the Save As Template button to save the current categories as a template, to provide categories automatically for future cookbooks

To add a category to an existing cookbook:

1. Open the cookbook to which you wish to add a category or categories.

2. Choose Edit Categories from the File menu (Categories on the Macintosh File menu).

    The Assign Categories dialog box appears (the Categories dialog box on a Macintosh).

3. For each category that you wish to add to the cookbook, type the category name and then click the Add button.

    As you add each category, it appears in alphabetical order in the list box.

> ▶ **NOTE:** You can avoid entering a cookbook's categories one at a time by using the current category template. See "To use the Category Template with a new cookbook," later in this section.

To remove a category from a cookbook:

1. Open the cookbook from which you wish to remove a category or categories.

2. Choose Edit Categories from the File menu (Categories on the Macintosh File menu).

    The Assign Categories dialog box appears (the Categories dialog box on a Macintosh).

3. Type the name for the category that you wish to remove from the cookbook or click the category name in the list.

4. Click the Delete button (the Remove button on a Macintosh).

    The category is deleted.

▶ **NOTE:** If a category has any recipes assigned to it when you attempt to delete it, a dialog box will appear to warn you that the category contains recipes and asking to confirm that you wish to delete it. If you still want to delete the category, deleting it will not harm your recipes.

To rename a category :

1. Open the cookbook containing the category or categories that you wish to rename and choose Categories from the File menu.

    The Categories dialog box appears.

2. Type the name for the category you wish to rename or click the category name in the list.

3. Click the Rename button.

    The Rename dialog box appears, containing a text box where you type the new name.

4. Type a new name for the category and then click the Rename button.

    The category is renamed.

To save a cookbook's categories as a template for future cookbooks:

1. Open the cookbook containing the category or categories you wish to use as a template, and choose Categories from the File menu.

    The Categories dialog box appears.

2. Click the Save as Template button.

    A dialog box appears, asking you to confirm that you want the current cookbook's categories saved as the new Category Template.

3. Click the Yes button.

    The categories are saved as the new template. The next time you create a cookbook, you can automatically assign it the template's categories without having to enter them again.

To use the Category Template with a new cookbook:

1. Create a new cookbook with the New Cookbook command.

2. When the Categories dialog box appears, click the Use Template button.

    The template categories appear in the Categories list box.

3. Add new categories or remove categories until you have the categories you wish to use; then click the OK button.

    When you click OK, the categories displayed in the Categories list box become the categories for the new cookbook.

Exporting Recipes from a Cookbook

The Export Selected Recipes command on the Recipe menu lets you export MasterCook recipes to text files, which can then be edited with a word processor or page layout program. (Note, however, that MasterCook probably won't be able to import an export file once it's been substantially modified by another program.) In addition, these text files can be uploaded to online services that require text file uploads, and subsequently downloaded by other users.

The Macintosh version of MasterCook offers two export formats: the *Mac* format, which is best suited for use with other Macintosh applications such as page layout programs and word processors; and the *MXP /Universal* format, which works better for posting recipes to online services, for sending in electronic mail, and for exchanging recipes with users of MasterCook for Windows.

To Export Recipes from a Cookbook:

1. In the cookbook window (or Recipe Clipboard), click the names of the recipes that you wish to export.

> ▶ **NOTE:** To select more than one recipe at a time, hold down the CONTROL key (COMMAND on a Macintosh) while clicking recipe names. You can make multiple contiguous selections by clicking the first recipe name, then holding down the SHIFT key while clicking the last recipe in your selection.

2. Choose Export Selected Recipes from the Recipe menu or click the Export button on the Control Bar.

Type an export file name here ⸻

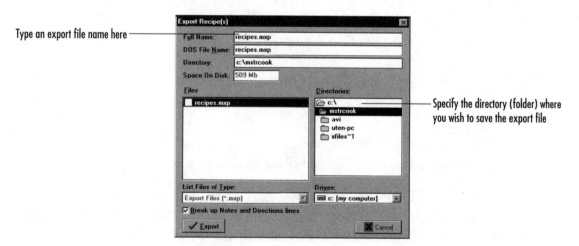

⸻ Specify the directory (folder) where you wish to save the export file

3. On a Macintosh only, choose an export format by clicking the appropriate radio button for either the *Mac* format or the *MXP/Universal* format.

Chapter 3

4. Type a name for the export text file.

5. Click the Export button.

   The selected recipes are exported to the specified text file.

Importing Recipes into a Cookbook

With the Import Recipes command, MasterCook lets you import recipes that have been exported to text files from MasterCook (see "Exporting Recipes from a Cookbook," the previous section) and other popular recipe programs, such as MealMaster™.

You can also use the Import Recipes command to import recipes received in electronic mail or downloaded from bulletin boards, online services, and World Wide Web pages.

▶ **NOTE:** Although MasterCook's Import Recipes command is very flexible and supports many different export formats, it cannot easily import recipes that are unformatted, such as those scanned from magazines or newspapers. All recipes should be formatted in a recognizable format for the Import Recipes command to work.

To Import Recipes into a Cookbook:

1. With a cookbook open, choose Import Recipes from the File menu.

   A dialog box appears to let you choose the file from which you wish to import recipes.

2. If the file from which you wish to import isn't listed in the Files list box, choose the appropriate directory (folder) and/or drive containing the file.

3. Click the name of the file containing the recipes that you wish to import and then click the Import button, or double-click the name of the file.

   The file is scanned and a list of recipes available for importing is displayed.

4. Click the names of the recipes you wish to import or click the Select All button to import all recipes in the file.

5. Click OK to import the selected recipes.

   The recipes are converted and copied into the current cookbook.

▶ **NOTE:** When an error is detected during import, the recipes affected are displayed in the Import Results Window. When a duplicate recipe is encountered (a recipe in the import file has the same name as one in the cookbook), a number is appended to the recipe name. Errors within the ingredients portion of a recipe are marked with a bullet (the "•" character) next to the offending line.

When you're finished importing recipes, click the Cancel button.

Copying Recipes from One Cookbook to Another

MasterCook lets you move recipes from one cookbook to another quickly and easily. One method of doing this is to use the Copy Selected Recipe(s) on the Edit menu to place recipes on the clipboard, and then use the Paste Recipe(s) command to place the recipe into a different cookbook. (See "Cutting, Copying, and Pasting Recipes" in Chapter Four, "Recipes," for more information.) The easiest way to copy recipes, however, is to use drag and drop.

1. With two cookbooks open and their cookbook windows visible, select the recipes you want to copy by clicking on their names.

2. Drag the selection of recipes to the cookbook window of the cookbook you wish to copy to.

    As you move your selection onto the destination cookbook window, the cursor changes to an icon representing a group of documents (or to a rectangle on a Macintosh); you can drop the recipes on a category at the left side of the cookbook window, or onto the recipe list on the right side.

3. Release the mouse button to finish copying the recipes.

    The recipes are copied to the specified cookbook file.

Deleting a Group of Recipes from a Cookbook

MasterCook offers a number of ways to delete recipes. With a recipe window open, you can delete the current recipe using the Delete Current Recipe command on the Recipe menu. When you wish to delete a *group* of recipes from a cookbook, however, use the Delete Selected Recipes command.

To delete a group of recipes from a cookbook (PC only):

1. In the cookbook window (or Recipe Clipboard window), click on the names of the recipes that you wish to delete from the cookbook.

2. Choose Delete Selected Recipes from the Recipe menu or click the Delete icon-button on the Control Bar.

    A dialog box appears, asking you to confirm that you want to delete the group of selected recipes.

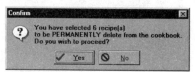

3. Click Yes to delete the recipes.

Chapter 3

To delete a group of recipes from a cookbook (Macintosh only):

1. In the cookbook window (or Recipe Clipboard window), click on the names of the recipes that you wish to delete from the cookbook.

2. Choose Delete Selected Recipes from the Recipe menu or click the Delete icon-button on the Control Bar.

   A dialog box appears, asking you to confirm that you want to delete the group of selected recipes.

3. To delete recipes selectively, click the Delete button to delete one recipe at a time.

   This way you can click Cancel if you have inadvertently selected a recipe that you don't wish to delete.

4. To delete the entire selection of recipes, click the Delete All button.

Printing a Cookbook

Before you print with MasterCook for the first time, it's a good idea to use the Page Setup command to specify your paper size and page orientation preferences.

To print a cookbook (PC Only):

1. Click on the cookbook window to make it the current active window.

2. Choose the Print Cookbook command from the File menu.

   A dialog box appears. The Print Cookbook dialog box contains a number of options to allow you to print a selection of recipes.

To print a selection of recipes rather than the entire cookbook, select the recipes that you wish to print. To select a category (or group of categories) for printing, click the category name(s) in the Categories list on the left side of the dialog. All the recipes in the selected category or categories will appear in the Recipes list on the right. Then click on the names of the recipes you wish to print in the recipes list on the right. Click Select All to print all recipes.

To select a contiguous group of categories, hold down the SHIFT key as you click on the first and last category names in the group. To select a noncontiguous group of categories, hold down the COMMAND key as you click on each category name.

3. If you wish, click Setup to choose different fonts, sizes, and styles; to choose a different recipe design; or to choose different page sizes (if you want to print the recipes as a book or as 3 x 5 or 4 x 6 recipe cards, for example).

4. Choose the printing options you want by clicking on the appropriate check boxes:

   - Complete Recipes — Prints each recipe in full.

   - Recipe Index — Prints an alphabetized listing of all selected recipes, along with their page numbers (if page numbering is selected).

   - Category Index — Prints an alphabetized listing of all categories.

   - Recipe Names by Category — Prints an alphabetized listing of all selected recipes, organized by category, along with their page numbers (if page numbering is selected).

   - Print Title Page — Prints a title page for the cookbook.

   - Start Recipes on New Page — When selected, MasterCook prints only one recipe per page. When deselected, MasterCook will print as many recipes as will fit on each page.

   - Number Pages — Prints page numbers and the cookbook name at the bottom of each printed page.

   - Include Nutrition — Prints a per-serving nutritional analysis of each recipe. Click Complete to include all nutritional information; click Brief to include only those nutrition items most commonly used (fat grams, % calories from fat, cholesterol, etc.).

5. To see how your recipes will look when printed, click the Print Preview button.

6. Click the Print button.

The selected recipes and/or indices are printed with the options you specified.

Chapter 3

To print a cookbook or multiple recipes (Macintosh only):

1. Click on the cookbook window to make it the current active window.

2. If you wish to print a selection of recipes rather than the entire cookbook, select the recipes that you wish to print in the cookbook window.

   To select a category (or group of categories) for printing, click the category name(s) in the categories list on the left side of a cookbook window. All the recipes in the selected category or categories will appear in the recipes list on the right. Then click on the names of the recipes you wish to print in the recipes list on the right.

   To select a contiguous group of categories, hold down the SHIFT key as you click on the first and last category names in the group.

   To select a noncontiguous group of categories, hold down the COMMAND key as you click on each category name.

3. Choose the Print Cookbook command from the File menu, or click the Print icon-button on the Control Bar.

   A dialog box appears. The Print Cookbook dialog box contains a number of options to allow you to print a selection of recipes in cookbook or recipe card form.

4. Click the appropriate radio button to choose whether to print the Entire Cookbook (all recipes in the cookbook file) or just the recipes currently selected in the cookbook or Recipe Clipboard window.

5. Click on the appropriate radio button to choose whether to print the recipes as a book or as 3 x 5 or 4 x 6 recipe cards.

6. If you choose to print the recipes in book form, choose the printing options you want by clicking on the appropriate check boxes:

   - Recipes — Prints each recipe in full.
     - Include Nutrition — Prints a per-serving nutritional analysis of each recipe.
     - Include Daily Values — Prints per-serving Daily Values for each recipe.
     - Number Pages — Prints page numbers and the cookbook name at the bottom of each printed page.
     - Start Recipes on New Page — When selected, MasterCook prints only one recipe per page. When deselected, MasterCook will print as many recipes as will fit on each page.
   - Title Page — Prints a title page for the cookbook.
   - Alphabetical Index — Prints an alphabetized listing of all selected recipes, along with their page numbers (if page numbering is selected).
   - Category Index — Prints an alphabetized listing of all selected recipes, organized by

category, along with their page numbers (if page numbering is selected).

If you choose to print the recipes in recipe card form, click the appropriate radio button to choose whether to feed the cards from the center or left side of the printer's paper feed.

7. Click the Print button.

    A second dialog box appears, to let you choose additional print options, including the number of copies, paper source, range of pages to print, and the font and type size with which to print the recipes.

8. Choose the additional print options you want and click the Print button.

    The selected recipes and/or indices are printed with the options you specified.

Printing the Recipe Clipboard

The Recipe Clipboard lets you group together any number of recipes in the current cookbook. You can place recipes on the Recipe Clipboard manually, by selecting them in the cookbook window, by dragging them with drag and drop, or with the Search Recipes command. You can then print any selection from the Recipe Clipboard that you wish — from one recipe to all the recipes on the Recipe Clipboard. This makes the Recipe Clipboard a handy "temporary storage area" for maintaining a group of recipes that you may wish to print all at one time.

To print the recipes in the Recipe Clipboard (PC only):

1. Click on the Recipe Clipboard window to make it the current active window, or choose Recipe Window from the Window menu.

2. To print all recipes on the Recipe Clipboard, choose Select All Recipes from the Edit menu; to print only a selection of recipes on the Recipe Clipboard, click on the names of those recipes that you wish to print.

3. Choose Print Selected Recipes from the File menu or click the Print icon-button on the Control Bar.

    The Print dialog box appears.

4. Choose the printing options you wish to use to print the selected recipes.

    See the preceding section, "Printing a Cookbook," for detailed information on cookbook printing options.

5. To see how your recipes will look when printed, click the Print Preview button.

6. Click the Print button.

    The selected recipes are printed with the specified options.

Chapter 3

To print the recipes in the Recipe Clipboard (Macintosh only):

1. Click on the Recipe Clipboard window to make it the current active window, or choose Recipe Window from the Window menu.

2. To print all recipes on the Recipe Clipboard, choose Select All Recipes from the Edit menu; to print only a selection of recipes on the Recipe Clipboard, click on the names of those recipes that you wish to print.

3. Choose Print Recipe Clipboard from the File menu on a Macintosh or click the Print icon-button on the Control Bar.

    The Print dialog box appears.

4. Choose the printing options you wish to use to print the selected recipes.

    See the preceding section, "Printing a Cookbook," for detailed information on cookbook printing options.

5. Click the Print button.

    The standard Print dialog box appears, containing additional print options, including the number of copies, paper source, range of pages to print, and the font and type size with which to print the recipes.

6. Choose the additional print options you want and click the Print button.

    The selected recipes are printed with the specified options.

4
RECIPES

Chapter 4

About Recipes

When you create a new recipe with MasterCook, it appears in its own window on the screen. Each recipe window supports two *views*: Edit View, which is designed to let you create and modify recipes as quickly as possible; and Page View, which displays the recipe as it will look when printed, allowing you to read the recipe more easily.

When it comes to printing your recipes, you can choose from a variety of print options. You can print on many different page sizes — from 3 x 5 recipe cards to legal size paper (8 ½ x 14) — and in any font, character style, and type size. You can also print a group of recipes or an entire cookbook, complete with title page and index. You can even print cookbooks as half-page booklets.

This chapter will tell you everything you need to know about storing, organizing, finding, and printing all your favorite recipes using MasterCook.

Opening Recipes from a Cookbook Window

A cookbook window lets you see at a glance all the categories and recipes in that cookbook, and lets you open the recipes you choose by just pointing and clicking. A cookbook window remains open for as long as the cookbook is open, although you can re-size it or move it to a different location on the screen if you choose.

Each cookbook window is divided into two lists — categories and recipes. The list on the left displays the categories in the cookbook like the chapter titles in a cookbook's table of contents; following each category name is a number indicating the number of recipes in that category. The list on the right contains the names of the recipes in the currently selected categories. At the top of the category list, in bold type, is the heading "All Recipes"; clicking on this heading displays all recipes in the cookbook in the recipes list at the right.

To open recipes from the cookbook window:

1. In the list of categories on the left side of the cookbook window, click on the names of the categories containing the recipes that you wish to open.

    As you click on each category name, the recipes associated with that category are displayed in the list on the right.

    To select a contiguous group of categories, hold down the SHIFT key and click on the first and last category names in the group. To select a noncontiguous group, hold down the CTRL key (COMMAND key on a Macintosh) and click the name of each category you want in the group. To display all recipes in the cookbook, click "All Recipes" at the top of the Categories list.

2. In the recipes list on the right, click on the names of the recipes that you wish to open.

    To select all recipes in a cookbook, choose Select All Recipes from the Edit menu.

As you click on each category name, the recipes in that category are displayed in the list of recipes on the right

To make a non-contiguous selection, hold down the CTRL key as you click each recipe you want to select

To select a contiguous group of recipes, hold down the SHIFT key and click on each recipe you want to select

3.   Click the Open button.

The selected recipes are opened in separate windows on the screen.

You can also open a single recipe by double-clicking its name in the recipe list.

▶   **NOTE:** MasterCook will open as many recipes as it has memory for. Windows will automatically allocate memory to the program as it needs it, but if you're using a Macintosh, you may want to increase the amount of memory allocated to MasterCook. To do this, select the MasterCook icon in the Finder, choose Get Info from the File menu, and type a larger number in the Preferred Size box (under the Memory Requirements heading).

Chapter 4

Opening Recipes with the Open Recipe Command

The Open Recipe command lets you open a recipe by choosing its name from a list or by typing its name.

To find a recipe by name:

1. Choose Open Recipe from the Recipe menu or click the Open Recipe icon-button on the Control Bar.

    A dialog box appears to let you type the name of the recipe you wish to open.

    The Open Recipe dialog box in the Windows version of MasterCook, like the cookbook window, displays a list of cookbooks on the left and a list of recipes on the right. The cookbooks list is the list of all open cookbooks in your MasterCook directory (the directory in which you installed MasterCook), along with all cookbooks in any directories contained in the MasterCook directory.

    If you click the checkbox titled "Include Unopened Cookbooks," the list displays all cookbooks in the MasterCook directory and all cookbooks in all directories contained in the MasterCook directory.

    The Open Recipe dialog box in the Macintosh version of MasterCook displays only those recipes in opened cookbooks.

2. In the text box above the Recipes list, type the name of the recipe that you wish to open.

    Below the recipe name that you're typing is an alphabetized list box containing the names of all recipes in the current cookbook. As you type, the list automatically scrolls to the name of the recipe in the cookbook most like the one you're typing.

    You can also scroll the list until you see the name of the recipe that you wish to open and then click the recipe name.

Type the name of the recipe you wish to open here

Click the Open button to open the selected recipe

3. Click the Open button.

Searching for Recipes that Meet Your Requirements

MasterCook's Search Recipes command lets you look for recipes in one or more cookbooks that match almost any criteria you can think of — ingredients, categories, recipe name, source of recipe, preparation time, cost per serving, and a variety of nutrition criteria. You can even do a "total recipe search" by specifying a word or phrase that appears anywhere in a recipe.

The Windows version of MasterCook lets you search through the current cookbook, all open cookbooks, or all cookbooks in the MasterCook directory (and any subdirectories within the MasterCook directory). With the Macintosh version of MasterCook, you can search through the current cookbook, all open cookbooks, or all cookbooks on any disk drive connected to your Macintosh.

What's more, you can search for recipes using almost any combination of recipe requirements. For example, you could tell MasterCook to find all recipes that: contain shrimp, garlic, and rice; are in the Italian or Chinese categories; take less than 45 minutes to prepare; begin with the name "Garlic Shrimp"; come from *The Healthy Heart Cookbook*; and are less than 30% fat.

The Search Recipes dialog box lets you build *search lines*, which are like sentences telling MasterCook what you're looking for in a recipe. You can combine as many search lines as you wish to create your own search criteria so that you can be as general or as specific as you want when looking for recipes.

Each search line consists of three components:
- the **part** of the recipe you want to search
- the **type** of search to be done
- **what** you want to search for

The chart on the next two pages describes the types of search lines that you can build. When used to describe the types of searches that may be made, the word "phrase" means "a part of a word, a single word, or several words." The graphic below illustrates the parts of the Search Recipes dialog box where you create and edit search lines.

As you build your search lines, you place them in this list box by clicking the Add

To create a search line:
(1) choose the *part* of the recipe you want to search...
(2) then choose the *kind* of search you want to do...
(3) and finally, specify *what* you wish to search for

Click to choose whether to search for recipes that meet *all* your criteria or for recipes that meet *any* of your requirements

Click to add the search line to your Search Criteria

Chapter 4

Part of Recipe	Type of Search	What You Can Search For	Instructions for Creating the Search Line
RECIPE	contains all of these	Searches for recipes that contain the specified phrase(s) *anywhere* in the recipe (nutrition information is not part of the recipe). MasterCook will look for recipes that contain *all* of the phrases (phrase 1 *and* phrase 2 *and* phrase 3, etc.).	Type the phrase(s) you wish to search for in the third list box. Separate phrases with semicolons.
	contains any of these	Searches for recipes that contain the specified phrase(s) *anywhere* in the recipe (nutrition information is not part of the recipe). MasterCook will look for recipes that contain *any* of the phrases (phrase 1 *or* phrase 2 *or* phrase 3, etc.).	Type the phrase(s) you wish to search for in the third list box. Separate phrases with semicolons.
	does not contain	Searches for recipes that do not contain the specified phrase(s).	Type in the third list box the phrase(s) you *don't* want the recipe(s) to contain. Separate phrases with semicolons.
Ingredients	include all of these	Searches for recipes that contain *all* the specified ingredients (ingredient 1 *and* ingredient 2 *and* ingredient 3, etc.).	Type the ingredients to search for in the third list box. Ingredient names can be partial names — you don't have to specify the full ingredient name. Separate ingredient names with semicolons.
	include any of these	Searches for recipes that contain *any* of the specified ingredients (ingredient 1 *or* ingredient 2 *or* ingredient 3, etc.).	Type the ingredients to search for in the third list box. Ingredient names can be partial names — you don't have to specify the full ingredient name. Separate ingredient names with semicolons.
	start with	Searches for recipes that begin with the specified ingredient name (or part of name).	Type the characters that the ingredient starts with.
	do not contain	Searches for all recipes that do not contain the specified ingredients.	Type in the third list box the ingredients you *don't* want the recipes to contain. Ingredient names can be partial names — you don't have to specify the full ingredient name. Separate ingredient names with semicolons.
Categories	include	Searches for all recipes that are in *any or all* of the categories specified — category 1 *and/or* category 2 *and/or* category 3, etc.	Choose categories by clicking on them in the third list box. To select a contiguous group, hold down the SHIFT key as you click on the first and last categories in the group. To select a non-contiguous group, hold down the COMMAND key as you click on each category.
	exclude	Searches for all recipes that are not in *any* of the categories specified.	Choose categories by clicking on them in the third list box. To select a contiguous group, hold down the SHIFT key as you click on the first and last categories in the group. To select a non-contiguous group, hold down the COMMAND key as you click on each category.

Part of Recipe	Type of Search	What You Can Search For	Instructions for Creating the Search Line
Recipe Name	contains all of these	Searches for recipes that contain in their names *all* the phrases specified.	Type in the third list box the phrases you want the recipe name to include. Separate phrases with semicolons.
	contains any of these	Searches for recipes that contain in their names *any* of the phrases specified.	Type in the third list box the phrases you want the recipe name to include. Separate phrases with semicolons.
	does not contain	Searches for recipes that do not contain the specified phrase(s) in their names.	Type in the third list box the phrases you want the recipe name to exclude. Separate phrases with semicolons.
	starts with	Searches for recipes with names that begin with the specified phrase.	Type the phrase that you want the recipe name to start with.
Recipe By	contains all of these	Searches for recipes that contain in their Recipe By fields *all* the phrases specified.	Type the name (or parts of the name) of the recipe source (the Recipe By field) you wish to search for in the third list box. Separate phrases with semicolons.
	contains any of these	Searches for recipes that contain in their Recipe By fields *any* of the phrases specified.	Type the name(s) of the recipe source(s) — the Recipe By field — you wish to search for in the third list box. Separate phrases with semicolons.
	does not contain	Searches for recipes that do not contain the specified phrases in their Recipe By fields.	Type in the third list box the recipe source(s) that you *don't* want the recipe to contain. Separate phrases with semicolons.
	starts with	Searches for recipes with Recipe By fields that begin with the specified phrase.	Type the phrase you want the recipe source (the Recipe By field) to start with.
Preparation Time	greater than	Searches for recipes with preparation times greater than the minimum specified.	Type a minimum preparation time. Use a ":" to separate hours and minutes (for example, if you just enter "1", it will accept it as "0:01").
	less than	Searches for recipes with preparation times less than the maximum specified.	Type a maximum preparation time. Use a ":" to separate hours and minutes.
	between	Searches for recipes with preparation times between the minimum and maximum specified.	Type a minimum preparation time (use a ":" to separate hours and minutes) and press TAB; then type a maximum preparation time.
Cost Per Serving	greater than	Searches for recipes that have a per-serving cost greater than the minimum specified.	Type a minimum value for per-serving cost..
	less than	Searches for recipes that have a per-serving cost less than the maximum specified.	Type a maximum value for per-serving cost..
	between	Searches for recipes with a cost between the minimum and maximum values specified.	Type minimum and maximum values for per-serving cost.
Nutrition Per Serving	greater than	Searches for recipes that have a value greater than the minimum specified for the selected nutrient/nutrition item.	Click on the appropriate nutrition item in the list on the left (Calories, Protein, etc.). Type a minimum value for the selected nutrition item.
	less than	Searches for recipes that have a value less than the maximum specified for the selected nutrient/nutrition item.	Click on the appropriate nutrition item in the list on the left (Calories, Protein, etc.). Type a maximum value for the selected nutrition item.
	between	Searches for recipes that have a value between the minimum and maximum values specified for the selected nutrient/nutrition item.	Click on the appropriate nutrition item in the list on the left (Calories, Protein, etc.). Type minimum and maximum values for the selected item.

Chapter 4

To search for recipes that match your requirements:

1. Choose Search Recipes from the Recipe menu or click the Search Recipes icon-button on the Control Panel.

    A dialog box appears.

2. In the first list box — on the bottom left — click on the *part* of the recipe to search.

3. In the second list box — in the middle — click on the *type* of search you want to perform.

4. In the third list box — on the bottom right — tell MasterCook *what* you want to look for.

    Except for searches made by categories (where you click on the names of the categories you wish to select), this means typing the phrases that you want to search for. *Separate words or phrases by typing semicolons (the ";" character) between them.*

5. Click the Add Line button to add the search line to the search criteria list at the top of the Search Recipes dialog box.

    You can repeat steps 2 through 5 above to add as many search lines to the search criteria list box as you like.

    To remove a search line from the Search Criteria list box, click on the line and then click the Delete Line button (the Remove button on a Macintosh). To remove *all* search lines from the Search Criteria list box, click the Clear Search button (Remove All on a Macintosh).

    To edit a search line, click on the line, click the Edit Line button, and then change the line as you see fit. When you're finished editing, click the Save Line button.

6. Click the appropriate radio button in the Match box — "All of these" or "Any of these."

    This box tells MasterCook what logic you want to use in combining the search lines. Specify whether you want MasterCook to search for all recipes that satisfy the require-ments of *all the search lines* in the search criteria box — by clicking "All of these" — or *any* of the search lines — by clicking "Any of these."

7. Indicate which cookbooks you want to search in the list labeled "From": All Open Cookbooks, All Available Cookbooks, or Selected Cookbooks.

    If you choose All Available Cookbooks, MasterCook will search through all cookbooks in the MasterCook directory as well as in all directories the MasterCook directory contains. On a Macintosh all cookbooks on all available disk drives are searched.

    To search Selected Cookbooks, choose the cookbooks you want to search from the bottom of the list. All cookbooks in the MasterCook directory (as well as in all directories the MasterCook directory contains) are displayed in this list. On a Macintosh, only open cookbooks are displayed on this list.

8.   Click the appropriate radio button to choose whether you want the list of recipes found during your search to be added to the Recipe Clipboard or to replace the Recipe Clipboard — or if you want the search to be performed only with those recipes already on the Recipe Clipboard.

9.   Click the Search button.

MasterCook displays a dialog box telling you the progress of the search as it looks through the cookbook for recipes meeting your specifications.

If no recipes are found, MasterCook displays a dialog box telling you that it didn't find any recipes matching your criteria. When you click OK, MasterCook returns to the Search Recipes dialog box, to let you try different search criteria. Perform a new search or click Cancel to close the Search Recipes dialog box.

If recipes matching your criteria are found, MasterCook closes the Search Recipes dialog box and displays the Recipe Clipboard, which contains a list of all recipes found.

The Recipe Clipboard window displays the names of recipes meeting your search criteria

Click on the recipes you want to look at, and then click the Open button to display them

Click on the recipes on the Recipe Clipboard that appeal to you and then click the Open button. MasterCook opens the selected recipes. The Recipe Clipboard contains the results of your search until your next search so that you can return to it to open additional recipes.

To print recipes on the Recipe Clipboard, click on the names of the recipes that you wish to print — or choose Select All Recipes from the Edit menu — and then choose Print Selected Recipes from the File menu (or click the Print icon-button on the Control Bar). See "Printing the Recipe Clipboard" in Chapter Three, "Cookbooks," for additional information.

Chapter 4

▶ **NOTE:** MasterCook automatically saves your search criteria so that you can do successive searches without having to repeatedly re-enter your search requirements. If you don't want MasterCook to save your search criteria, you can deactivate this feature with the Preferences command on the Tools menu. See "Setting MasterCook Preferences" in Chapter Eight, "Tools."

Creating a New Recipe

Creating recipes is perhaps the single most important task performed by MasterCook, and, because of the many options offered by the program, it calls for a particularly detailed discussion. For this reason, this section is divided into the following groups of procedures:

- Creating, naming, and saving a new recipe
- Entering basic recipe information
- Specifying categories for a recipe
- Entering ingredients
- The Ingredients List and nutritional information
- Typing directions
- Recipe options

To create, name, and save a new recipe:

1. Choose New Recipe from the Recipe menu, or click the New Recipe icon-button on the Control Bar.

    A new recipe window appears and is temporarily named "New Recipe 1" ("Untitled Recipe" on a Macintosh).

Click and drag an ingredient's row number to move it up or down in the list

Click these tabs to move between the Directions, Notes, and Categories text areas

Click and drag this splitter bar to resize the Ingredients and tab areas relative to one another. Drag up to reduce the Ingredients area and increase the size of the tab areas; drag down to increase the Ingredients area and reduce the size of the tab areas.

2. Type the name of the recipe in the Recipe Name text box.

3. Click the Save button.

The recipe is saved on disk as part of the current cookbook. The recipe's name is added in the cookbook window to each category to which you assign it and its name appears in the recipe window's title bar.

As you work on a recipe, you can save it at any time by clicking the Save button (or pressing COMMAND-S on a Macintosh).

To enter basic recipe information:

1. Press TAB to move to the Recipe By text box.

2. Type the name of the recipe's author.

The Recipe By text box lets you record the source of the recipe. For example, you can use this area to record the name of the cook who created the recipe, the cookbook it came from, or the magazine it appeared in. You can also set the option in the Preferences dialog box (accessed from the Tools menu) that uses the last saved author in new recipes.

3. Press TAB to move to the Serves text box (Servings on a Macintosh).

4. Type the number of servings the recipe makes.

▶ **NOTE:** The Serves and Prep Time text boxes (Servings and Preparation Time on a Macintosh) won't accept any characters other than numbers and special characters — such as the colon (":"), which is used to separate hours and minutes in the Prep Time text box.

MasterCook uses this number to adjust the ingredient amounts for a variable number of servings (up to 999). In most recipes, the servings amount is the number of individuals the recipe serves. In some recipes, however, this number indicates the number of units produced: loaves, cakes, pies, etc.

Note, however, that some recipes, particularly those for breads, were not intended by their authors to be scaled. If you are creating a recipe that you feel shouldn't be scaled, use the Notes text box to indicate that the number of servings for the recipe should not be altered.

5. Press TAB to move to the Prep Time text box (Preparation Time on a Macintosh).

6. Type, in hours and minutes, the amount of time required to prepare the recipe.

To designate hours, type a number followed by a colon; otherwise, MasterCook will assume only minutes are intended and will convert the time to hours and minutes based on the number of minutes. For example, if you type "3:00," the preparation time will be three hours and no minutes; but if you type "300," MasterCook will assume that you mean 300 minutes and will convert it to five hours and no minutes ("5:00").

Chapter 4

You don't have to specify the amount of preparation time. If you don't enter a preparation time, the default time of zero hours and minutes will be used.

To specify categories for a recipe:

1. On a PC, click the Categories tab or press ALT-C to display the names of all the categories in the current cookbook.

    On a Macintosh, click the Categorize button or press COMMAND-K to display a dialog box showing all of the categories in the current cookbook.

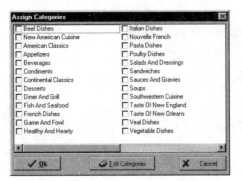

2. Click the check box beside each appropriate category name.

    You can choose up to 10 categories for any one recipe. In the cookbook window, Master-Cook will display the recipe's name under each category you assign to it.

▶ **NOTE:** If you wish to add or change a category as you work: on a PC, choose Edit Categories from the File menu; on a Macintosh, click the Edit Categories button. The Categories dialog box appears, allowing you to add to or modify categories in the current cookbook. Click the OK button to save your category changes and exit the dialog box.

To enter ingredients for a recipe:

The area below the recipe name and author is where you'll enter the recipe's ingredients. This Ingredients list box is set up in tabular form, containing the amount, measurement unit, the ingredient name and how you want the ingredient prepared prior to cooking. You'll repeat the steps below for each ingredient you enter in a recipe.

1. Press TAB to move to the Amount column and type the amount of the ingredient.

    You can type either decimal or fractional amounts. If you're using the default number display for amounts, Common Fractions, the amount will be converted to a common household fractional amount: eighths, fourths, thirds, or halves. If you've used the Preferences command on the Tools menu to change the display to show decimal numbers, the amounts will appear in decimal form with the number of decimal places you specified.

2. Press TAB to move to the Unit column and type a measurement unit.

    As you begin typing, a drop-down list of standard units appears; the list automatically scrolls to highlight the name most like the letters you're typing. Note that this name appears in the text box as well, with a portion of the name you didn't type highlighted. This is MasterCook's *fast-fill* feature: as you type, MasterCook instantly "fills in" the text box with the name of the unit that it "guesses" you want, based on the letters typed so far. The portion of the unit name you didn't type appears selected, meaning you can continue typing to specify a different unit.

    If the fast-fill unit name is the one you want, you can just press TAB to move to the next column. If it's not, you can click on another unit name in the list or continue typing to find a different standard unit. If you wish to use a nonstandard measurement unit — one not in the list — just type any nonstandard name you wish.

▶ **NOTE:** A nonstandard unit name is treated as a "whole" for nutritional information. For example, if you type "stick" to indicate a stick of butter, MasterCook will assume that you mean a whole unit of butter in stick form when it calculates nutritional information for the recipe.

---

3. Press TAB to move to the Ingredient column and type the name of the ingredient.

    As you type the ingredient name, a drop-down list appears below it, showing you an extensive list of food items maintained by MasterCook for the purpose of providing nutritional information (known as the *Ingredients List*). The item most like the one you're typing appears highlighted in the list and, as with the measurement units, appears "fast-filled" in the text box where you're typing.

Chapter 4

▶ **NOTE:** Some of the items in the list appear in bold type; these are the items in the Ingredients List whose volume nutritional information is maintained in whole quantities (such as an egg, a slice of bread, a whole banana) rather than in standard volume measurement units (cups, liters, tablespoons, etc.). When you choose such an item, make sure that you specify either a whole unit or a weight unit in the Unit column, or the nutritional analysis for the recipe may be inaccurate.

If the fast-fill ingredient is not the one you're looking for, click another one on the list or continue typing the ingredient name. To enter an ingredient not on the Ingredients List, just type any name you wish. You won't be asked to provide additional information about this ingredient unless you create a nutritional analysis of the recipe, at which time MasterCook will warn you that no nutritional information exists for the ingredient.

You may want to use an ingredient name not on the Ingredients List that nevertheless describes an item for which MasterCook maintains nutritional information, or you may wish to assign the nutritional values of a similar food to an ingredient. To do so, see "Recipe Ingredients and Nutritional Information," in this chapter.

4. Press TAB to move to the Prep Time column (Preparation Time on a Macintosh) and type any relevant information about how the ingredient should be prepared prior to cooking.

As you type the preparation method, a drop-down list of preparation methods maintained by MasterCook appears below it. The item most like the one you're typing appears highlighted in the list; it also appears "fast-filled" in the area where you're typing. If you type a name not already in the list, it will be added to MasterCook's list of preparation methods when you save the recipe.

To enter recipe directions:

1. On a PC, click the Directions tab or press ALT-D to display the Directions text box.

   On a Macintosh, press TAB to move to the Directions text box.

   You can change how the Directions box is displayed on a Macintosh — either as a text box or as a separate window — with the Preferences command on the Tools menu.

2. Type the recipe's directions.

   Type in the Directions text box as you would in a word processor. You can type up to 10,000 characters' worth of directions for each recipe.

3. When you're finished, save the recipe.

To enter recipe options (Suggested Wine, Serving Ideas, Notes):

The Suggested Wine, Serving Ideas, and Notes text areas are optional features intended to increase the flexibility and usefulness of MasterCook.

1. Press TAB to move to the Suggested Wine text box and then type a wine suggestion.

2. Press TAB to move to the Serving Ideas text box and type serving ideas — other foods or recipes to serve with the recipe.

    For example, if you have a two-part recipe — such as a meat dish served with a certain sauce — you may want to divide it into two recipes and use the Serving Ideas area in each recipe to store a reference to the companion recipe.

3. On a PC, click the Notes tab to open the Notes text area and type your notes.

    On a Macintosh, press TAB to move to the Notes text box and type notes for the recipes as you would in a word processor.

    For example, you might want to note special instructions for the recipe or information about the restaurant or cookbook where the recipe originated. The Notes area can store up to 1,000 characters.

Recipe Ingredients and Nutritional Information

You may wish to use an ingredient name not on the Ingredients List that nevertheless describes an item for which MasterCook maintains nutritional information. For example, you might be typing a recipe that calls for "Grecian laurel leaves or bay leaves." MasterCook doesn't have nutritional information for Grecian laurel leaves, but it does for bay leaves. What you'd like to do is enter the recipe exactly as written by its chef but still use the nutritional data for bay leaves.

Or, you may wish to assign the nutritional values of a similar food to an ingredient, such as assigning the nutritional values for vinegar to a flavored vinegar not on the Ingredients List, which creates a practical approximation of the recipe's nutritional content.

MasterCook lets you create just such an association, called a *link*. Furthermore, MasterCook offers a variety of convenient and easy ways to link ingredients and nutritional data. MasterCook also lets you display a nutritional analysis of an ingredient in the recipe window so that you can check on an ingredient's nutritional content even as you enter it.

Chapter 4

To create a nutritional link for an ingredient:

1. In the recipe's Ingredient column, click on the name of the ingredient for which you wish to create a nutritional link and choose Link With Ingredient from the Edit menu.

   The Nutritional Link dialog box appears, containing the Ingredients List.

Type the name of the ingredient for which you wish to create a link...

...or click its name in the list

```
┌─────────────────────────────────────────┐
│ Link With Ingredient              [ X ]  │
├─────────────────────────────────────────┤
│ bay leaf                                 │
├─────────────────────────────────────────┤
│ bass fillet                          ▲   │
│ bass fillets                             │
│ bass, freshwater                         │
│ bass, striped                            │
│ bay leaf                                 │
│ bay leaves                               │
│ bay scallops                             │
│ bay shrimp                               │
│ bay shrimp, cooked                   ▼   │
├─────────────────────────────────────────┤
│  ✓  OK          │      X  Cancel         │
└─────────────────────────────────────────┘
```

   If a link has already been made for the ingredient, the linked Ingredients List food item appears highlighted in the list and is displayed in the text box above the list. Otherwise, the item with the name most like the ingredient name you typed appears fast-filled in the text box.

2. Click the name of the food item with which you want to link the ingredient.

   Scroll the list if the appropriate item is not in view, or type the name of the food item in the text box above the list.

3. Click the Link button.

   The link is made. The ingredient appears in italic type to indicate that it is an ingredient with a nutritional link.

There may be times when you wish to remove a link from an ingredient.

To remove a nutritional link:

1. Select the ingredient name and choose Link with Ingredient from the Edit menu.

    The Nutritional Link dialog box appears, containing the Ingredients List. The linked Ingredients List food item appears highlighted in the text box above the list.

2. Press the BACKSPACE or DELETE key.

    The link is removed.

3. Click the OK button.

    The link is removed. The ingredient appears in the regular (non-italic) typeface to indicate that it is an ingredient without a nutritional association.

To display the nutritional analysis of an ingredient in the recipe window:

■ Click on the name of the ingredient for which you wish to display a nutritional analysis and choose Ingredient Analysis from the Tools menu.

    The Ingredient Analysis dialog box appears, displaying nutritional information for the current ingredient.

▶ **NOTE:** The Ingredient Analysis dialog box also tells you what weight and volume measures the food item's nutritional information is based on, so you can create more accurate nutritional analyses.

Editing and Viewing Recipes

MasterCook supports multiple views of recipes, with two main kinds of views: Edit View — where you create and change a recipe — and Page View — which shows how a recipe will look when printed. Edit View makes it easy to create and modify recipes. Page View lets you read recipes quickly and see how they will look when printed. With Page View, you can also choose different Recipe Designs with which to view and print recipes.

Page View is implemented differently in the Windows and Macintosh versions of Master-Cook. In the Windows version, you choose different Recipe Designs in a recipe window; in the Macintosh version, you choose different Recipe Designs in the cookbook window. The Macintosh version of MasterCook also lets you browse through a cookbook using different page layouts.

Chapter 4

Editing a Recipe

MasterCook gives you a good deal of freedom in editing your recipes — just open the recipe that you want to modify and make whatever changes you like. Once you save a recipe, however, your changes become permanent. If you want to add to or otherwise change a recipe but retain the old recipe information, first make a copy of the recipe using the Save Recipe As command. See "Making a Copy of a Recipe" and "Renaming a Recipe" in this chapter for information on making copies of recipes.

To edit a recipe:

1. Open the recipe from the cookbook window or locate it using the Open Recipe or Search Recipes commands.

2. Make your changes to the recipe.

   For complete information on working in a recipe window, see "Creating a New Recipe" in this chapter. For information on editing ingredient rows, see "Editing Ingredient Rows" also in this chapter.

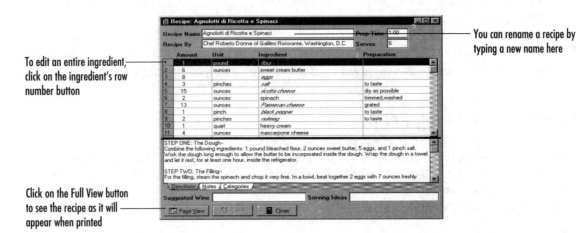

To edit an entire ingredient, click on the ingredient's row number button

You can rename a recipe by typing a new name here

Click on the Full View button to see the recipe as it will appear when printed

3. Click the Save button to save your changes.

   To close the recipe without saving your changes, click the recipe's close box.

► **NOTE:** You can resize a recipe window in the Windows version of MasterCook as you would any window in the Window environment: drag any corner or side of the window. The window is resized and all parts of the window are resized proportionately. You can also resize the parts of a recipe window occupied by the Ingredient area and the Directions, Notes, and Categories areas (in Edit View): just click on the black line separating the two areas and drag up or down. If you drag down, the Ingredients area expands while the tab areas decrease; if you drag up, the Ingredients area shrinks as the tab areas increase.

Viewing a Recipe with Page View

Page View lets you view a recipe in the format with which it will be printed, rather than the editing format you see while in Edit View. Whereas Edit View is like looking at the ingredients of a recipe-in-progress on your kitchen counter, Page View is more like the meal you present to hungry guests: it's the finished product. When in Page View, recipes can be read quickly and easily, even from a distance — so if you use your computer in the kitchen, you can use Page View to see the recipe more clearly.

To display a recipe with Page View:

1. Open the recipe to be viewed.

2. Click the Page View button (the View button on a Macintosh).

    The recipe window changes to display the recipe as it will appear when printed, using the current Recipe Design.

    If you're using the Windows version of MasterCook, the recipe is displayed with the current Recipe Design, shown in the drop-down list box on the bottom-right of the screen. The Page View button changes to Edit.

    If you're running MasterCook on a Macintosh, the recipe is displayed using the current Recipe Design, and the cookbook window changes to the last Cookbook View used.

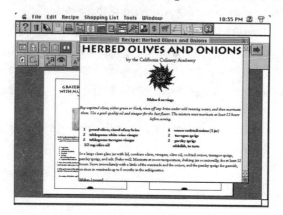

Chapter 4

3.   To return to Edit view, click the Edit button.

To change recipe designs (for viewing and printing):

■   On a PC, choose a Recipe Design from the Design list box in the lower-right part of the recipe window.

On a Macintosh, click on the recipe's cookbook window and choose a Recipe Design from the Recipe Design menu; then choose the recipe window from the Window menu.

Using Pictures in Recipes

If you're using MasterCook with the Cooking Light Digital Cookbook or MasterCook Deluxe, you've seen how MasterCook can display beautiful, high-resolution pictures alongside recipes. What you may not realize, however, is that you can also add pictures and graphics to your own recipes. The PC version of MasterCook lets you add any graphic or image in Windows bitmap format (.BMP) to a recipe, while the Macintosh version lets you paste PICT graphics copied from the Clipboard.

▶   **NOTE:** You can only add pictures to (and remove pictures from) recipes saved on your hard drive — cookbooks on CD-ROM cannot be modified.

To insert a picture into a recipe on a PC:

1.   Open the recipe to which you wish to add a picture.

2.   Choose Insert Picture from the Recipe menu.

3.   Select the picture file you wish to insert (Windows .BMP format only) and click the OK button.

A dialog box appears, offering several options that allow you to control picture scaling (the size and dimensions of your picture within the recipe):

• Original Size — places the picture in the recipe at its original size

• Scale to Page — shrinks or enlarges the picture to the maximum size available within the current page size (using the margins specified with Page Setup)

• Use Screen Resolution — scales the picture to the screen resolution of your video driver

• Custom — lets you choose custom sizes for the picture in inches or percentages of the picture's original size

4. Choose the option that suits your needs and click the OK button.

   You can change the scaling at any time by using the Scale Picture command on the Recipe menu.

   If you're in Page View and have a picture template selected, the picture will appear at full size; in Edit Mode, a thumbnail (small preview) will appear at the upper right corner of the recipe window.

> **NOTE:** Displaying large pictures may require large amounts of memory and having several recipe windows containing large pictures open at the same time may slow down MasterCook's performance slightly and cause delays. If your program seems to operate slowly, try closing one or more recipe windows.

To insert a picture into a recipe on a Macintosh:

Before inserting a picture into a recipe on a Macintosh, you must have a picture on the Macintosh Clipboard. This can be done by opening a graphics program or the Scrapbook, copying the picture to the Clipboard, and then returning to MasterCook. See your Macintosh User's Guide for more information on Clipboard operations.

1. Open the recipe to which you wish to add a picture.

   If in Page View, switch to Edit mode by clicking the Edit button.

2. Choose Paste from the Edit menu.

   A dialog box appears, providing two options:

   - Actual size (crop to fit) — places the picture in the recipe at its original size, trimming edges of the picture too large to fit within the margins of the recipe
   - Scale to fit — scales the picture to the maximum size permitted by the margins of the recipe

3. Choose the option that suits your needs and click the OK button.

   A thumbnail (small preview) will appear at the upper-right corner of the recipe window.

> **NOTE:** Displaying large pictures may require large amounts of memory and having several recipe windows containing large pictures open at the same time may slow down MasterCook's performance slightly and cause delays. If your program seems to operate slowly, try closing one or more recipe windows.

To remove a picture from a recipe:

- On a PC: with the recipe open, choose Remove Picture from the Recipe menu.

  On a Macintosh: with the recipe open, click on the thumbnail of the picture and choose Clear from the Edit menu.

Chapter 4

Cutting, Copying, and Pasting Text in Recipes

MasterCook fully supports the Macintosh text editing commands — Undo, Cut, Copy, Paste, Clear, and Select All — for creating and editing recipes.

To cut text in a recipe:

1. Select the text to be cut.

2. Choose Cut from the Edit menu or press CTRL-X (COMMAND-X on a Macintosh).

   The text is cut from the recipe and placed on the Clipboard. You can now move the cursor and insert the text elsewhere in this (or another) recipe with the Paste command.

To copy text:

1. Select the text to be copied.

2. Choose Copy from the Edit menu or press CTRL-C (COMMAND-C on a Macintosh).

   The text is copied to the Clipboard. The text can now be placed somewhere else in this — or another — recipe with the Paste command.

To paste text:

1. Place the cursor where you want the text to be pasted.

2. Choose Paste from the Edit menu or press CTRL-C (COMMAND-V on a Macintosh).

   The text is inserted following the cursor.

Editing Ingredient Rows

In order to make recipe entry quicker and easier, MasterCook breaks down recipe ingredients into components — amount, measurement unit, ingredient, and preparation method. But to a cook, an ingredient is the sum of all these components. Frequently you'll find that you want to delete an entire ingredient row at one time — not piece by piece. Or you'll want to insert an ingredient in between two that you've already typed. Or you may even want to grab three ingredients from Recipe A and place them in Recipe B.

Fortunately, MasterCook makes this easy because you can select entire ingredient rows at once and use the Clipboard commands (Cut, Copy, Paste) to edit them — just like you cut, copy, and paste text. You can also drag and drop ingredient rows both within a recipe and between recipes.

To edit an ingredient row, you first select the row by clicking on its row number button.

To edit an entire ingredient row, first click on the ingredient's row number button

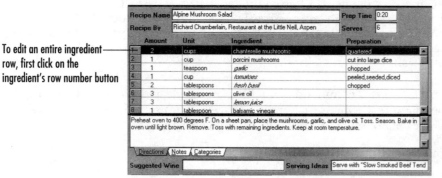

You can select multiple ingredient rows the same way you select multiple items in the cookbook window: to select a group of ingredients, click on the row number button for the first item, hold down the SHIFT key, and then click the row number button of the last ingredient in the group.

Chapter 4

To select a group of ingredients, hold down the SHIFT key, then click the row number buttons for the first and last ingredients in the group

Once you've selected the row(s) that you want to edit, choose the appropriate editing command. When a row or group of rows is selected, the usual Cut, Copy, and Clear commands are changed to Cut Row(s), Copy Row(s), and Clear Row(s) on the Edit menu. When you cut or copy a row to the Clipboard, the usual Paste command becomes Paste Row(s). Cut Row(s) removes all selected rows and places the row or rows on the Clipboard; Copy Row(s) copies all selected rows to the Clipboard; Paste Row(s) inserts a row from the Clipboard into a recipe; Clear Row(s) removes all selected rows from the recipe. (You can also use Delete Row(s) to remove a selection of rows.)

In addition to the usual Clipboard commands for editing rows, MasterCook's Edit menu includes a special command that applies to ingredient rows only: Insert Blank Row, which, as its name implies, inserts a blank row in front of the selected row.

To cut ingredient rows from a recipe:

1. Click on the appropriate ingredient row number(s) to select the ingredient(s) to be cut.

    The selected rows appear highlighted.

2. Choose Cut Row(s) from the Edit menu or press CTRL-X (COMMAND-X on a Macintosh).

    The selected ingredient rows are removed from the recipe and stored on the Clipboard.

    The Paste command on the Edit menu changes to Paste Row(s), to indicate that the Clipboard now contains an ingredient row or rows rather than just random text.

To copy ingredient rows to the Clipboard:

1. Click on the appropriate ingredient row number(s) to select the ingredient(s) to be copied.

    The selected ingredient rows are highlighted.

2. Choose Copy Row(s) from the Edit menu or press CTRL-C (COMMAND-C on a Macintosh).

    The selected ingredient rows are copied to the Clipboard. The ingredients remain unchanged in the original recipe.

The Paste command on the Edit menu changes to Paste Row(s), to indicate that the Clipboard now contains an ingredient row rather than just random text.

To paste ingredient rows into a recipe:

1. Select the place in the Ingredients section where you wish to paste the recipe.

   If you wish to have the ingredient row(s) on the Clipboard *replace* other ingredients, select the appropriate ingredients by clicking the row number(s) of the ingredients that you wish to replace.

   If you wish to *insert* the ingredient row(s) on the Clipboard *between other ingredients without modifying them,* click somewhere in the text of the ingredient line where you wish to insert the ingredient row(s).

2. Choose Paste Row(s) from the Edit menu or press CTRL-V (COMMAND-V on a Macintosh).

   If one or more ingredient rows are selected, they are replaced with the ingredient row(s) on the Clipboard. If the insertion point is selected within the text of an ingredient, the row or rows on the Clipboard are inserted in front of the ingredient row containing the insertion point.

To remove ingredient rows from a recipe:

1. Click on the appropriate ingredient row number(s) to select ingredient(s) to be deleted.

2. Choose Clear Row(s) from the Edit menu.

   The selected row or rows are removed from the recipe.

To insert a blank ingredient row into a recipe:

1. Click on the row number of the ingredient (or anywhere in the ingredient) where you wish to insert a blank ingredient row.

2. Choose Insert Blank Row from the Edit menu or press CTRL-I (COMMAND-I on a Macintosh).

   A blank ingredient row is inserted in front of the selected ingredient.

Chapter 4

Dragging and Dropping Ingredient Rows

In addition to cutting, copying, and pasting ingredient rows, you can also move ingredient rows with MasterCook's drag and drop feature. Drag and drop is very easy to use — just select a row by clicking on it and drag it to the place where you want to move it.

To drag and drop ingredient rows within a recipe:

1. Select the ingredient row that you wish to move.

2. Holding down the mouse button, drag the row to a new position in the recipe.

3. Release the mouse button.

    The ingredient row is inserted in front of the row where you release the mouse button.

▶   **NOTE:** You can drag and drop multiple ingredient rows as well as individual ones. Just make a multiple selection and drag the rows to the desired location.

Cutting, Copying, and Pasting Recipes

MasterCook lets you take full advantage of the Windows and Macintosh Clipboard editing features — the Cut, Copy, and Paste commands that give these graphical interfaces a common means of transferring data between files quickly and easily. With MasterCook, not only can you cut, copy, and paste text and ingredient rows, but you can also use the Clipboard editing commands on entire recipes. This section explains how to use the Clipboard commands to move and replace complete recipes.

When you cut or copy a recipe, the entire recipe is placed on the Clipboard, the portion of memory that your computer uses to store information that you plan to move from one area to another inside a file or between files. For example, you can use Cut Recipe and Copy Recipe to place a copy of a recipe on the Clipboard and then place the recipe into another cookbook file — or even into another program, such as Microsoft Word or Adobe PageMaker — with the Paste command.

To cut a recipe from a cookbook:

1. Open the recipe that you wish to cut.

2. Choose Cut Recipe from the Edit menu.

    A dialog box appears, warning that the Cut Recipe operation cannot be reversed with the Undo command and asking if you wish to proceed.

3. Click Yes to cut the recipe from the cookbook.

    The recipe is cut from the cookbook and placed on the Clipboard. You can now paste it into other cookbooks or into a different program such as a word processor.

▶ **NOTE:** Although Cut Recipe is not technically Undo-able, you can easily recover the recipe by choosing Paste Recipe from the Edit menu before performing any further cut or copy operations. When you choose Paste Recipe, the recipe on the Clipboard is "pasted" back into the Clipboard.

To copy a recipe to the Clipboard:

1. Open the recipe that you wish to copy to the Clipboard.

2. Choose Copy Recipe from the Edit menu.

    The recipe is copied onto the Clipboard; the original recipe is unaffected. You can now paste the copied recipe into the same or a different cookbook, or paste it as text into other programs.

To paste a recipe from the Clipboard:

Paste Recipe inserts the recipe on the Clipboard into the current cookbook. If no recipe has been cut from the Clipboard, this command is not available.

■   Choose Paste Recipe (Paste on a Macintosh) from the Edit menu.

    The recipe is pasted into the current cookbook and appears in its own window.

    If you attempt to paste a recipe into a cookbook that contains the original of the recipe — or a recipe with an identical name — MasterCook will display a dialog box, asking if you wish to replace it.

▶ **NOTE:** As with Cut Recipe, Paste Recipe is not Undo-able. Remove unwanted recipes with the Delete Selected Recipes command from the Recipe menu.

Dragging and Dropping Recipes

One of the ways MasterCook makes it easier than ever to manage your recipes is through the use of drag and drop. Imagine a cookbook where you can drag recipes from one chapter to another — or, better yet, imagine dragging recipes from one cookbook to another. This is exactly what MasterCook lets you do with drag and drop.

When you drag a recipe from one category to another within a single cookbook, the recipe is added to the second category (and, of course, the second category is added to the recipe's list of categories). When you drag a recipe from one cookbook to another, not only is the recipe added to the category in the second cookbook onto which you drag the recipe, but the recipe's categories are also added to the second cookbook so that no recipe information is lost.

Chapter 4

To drag and drop a recipe (or group of recipes) onto a new category in the same cookbook:

1. On the right side of the cookbook window, select the recipe or recipes that you wish to add to a new category.

2. Holding down the mouse button, drag the recipe(s) to the new category on the left side of the cookbook window.

3. Release the mouse button.

   The recipe(s) are added to the new category.

To drag and drop a recipe (or group of recipes) from one cookbook to another:

1. On the right side of the cookbook window, select the recipe or recipes that you wish to copy to the second cookbook.

2. Holding down the mouse button, drag the recipe(s) from the first cookbook window until they are positioned over the desired category in the second cookbook window.

   If you want to drag and drop recipes into a second cookbook but don't want to assign them all to a specific category, position them over the right (recipes) side of the cookbook window. The recipes (and their existing categories) will be added to the second cookbook but not to any particular category in that cookbook.

3. Release the mouse button.

   The recipe(s) are added to the new category.

Making a Duplicate of a Recipe

When you want to make a copy of a recipe, use the Save Recipe As command. Save Recipe As saves a copy of the recipe with a different name to the current cookbook. Use Save Recipe As when you want to make changes to a recipe but want to keep a copy of the recipe in its original form as well.

To duplicate a recipe:

1. Open the recipe that you want to duplicate.

2. Choose Save Recipe As from the Recipe menu.

    A dialog box appears, requesting a new name for the recipe.

3. Type a new name for the recipe and click the Save button.

    A copy of the recipe is saved with its new name to the current cookbook.

Renaming a Recipe

Renaming recipes in MasterCook is simple — just give it a new name and save it!

To rename a recipe:

1. Open the recipe you want to rename.

2. Type a new name for the recipe in the Recipe Name text box.

3. Click the Save button to save the recipe with its new name.

    The recipe is saved with its new name to the current cookbook. Its name is changed in the cookbook window, and the new name appears in the title bar of the recipe window.

Deleting Recipes

The Recipe menu contains a command for removing unwanted recipes from a cookbook: when you have a group of recipes selected in the cookbook window, this command is Delete Selected Recipes; when you have a recipe window open, this command becomes Delete Current Recipe.

To delete the current recipe:

1. Open the recipe you wish to delete.

2. Choose Delete Current Recipe from the Recipe menu or click the Delete icon-button on the Control Bar.

    A dialog box appears, asking you to confirm that you wish to permanently delete the recipe from the cookbook.

Chapter 4

3. Click Yes to delete the recipe.

    The recipe is permanently removed from the cookbook.

▶ **NOTE:** This operation cannot be reversed with the Undo command. Use with care!

To delete a group of recipes:

1. In the cookbook window, select the names of the recipes that you wish to delete.

2. Choose Delete Selected Recipes from the Recipe menu or click the Delete icon-button on the Control Bar.

    A dialog box appears, asking you to confirm that you wish to permanently delete the recipes from the cookbook.

3. Click Yes to delete the recipes.

    The recipes are permanently removed from the cookbook.

▶ **NOTE:** This operation cannot be reversed with the Undo command. Use with care!

Exporting Recipes to a Text File

MasterCook lets you export recipes to text files so that they can be used by other programs that read text files — such as word processors and page layout programs — and transferred over network services that require text file transfer, such as some e-mail systems and commercial on-line services. (Of course, the easiest way to send recipes over networks is with MasterCook's Mail Recipes command. See "Mailing Recipes," later in this chapter.)

▶ **NOTE:** Because the Export Recipe command exports recipes to MasterCook's export text format, you can import these exported recipes back into MasterCook by using the Import Recipes command on the File menu (see "Importing Recipes into a Cookbook," in Chapter Three, "Cookbooks").

MasterCook's exported text files can be read by any program that can read text files. However, don't modify an exported file with another program if you wish to import it back into MasterCook with the Import Recipes command — you may alter important formatting information.

To export the current recipe to a text file:

1. Make sure the recipe you want to export is the current active window.

2. Choose Export Recipe from the Recipe menu or click on the Export icon-button on the Control Bar.

    A dialog box appears, asking you to specify the file to which you wish to export the recipe.

3. To export the recipe to a file in a different directory (folder) or on a different disk-drive, select the appropriate directory or folder name in the Directories list box.

4. Type a file name for the recipe.

5. Click the Export button.

    The recipe is saved in a new text file with the name you specified.

To export a group of recipes to a text file:

1. In the cookbook window, select the recipes that you want to export.

2. Choose Export Selected Recipes from the Recipe menu or click on the Export icon-button on the Control Bar.

    A dialog box appears, asking you to specify the file to which you wish to export the recipes.

Chapter 4

Type a name for the export file here ──────

Export Recipe(s)

Full Name: Exported Text File
DOS File Name: EXPORTED.MXP
Directory: c:\mstrcook
Space On Disk: 705 Mb

Files

Directories:
📂 c:\
📁 mstrcook   ── If you wish, choose a new directory

List Files of Type: Drives:
Export Files (*.mxp)   💻 c: [my computer]   ── If you wish, choose a new disk drive
☑ Break up Notes and Directions lines

✓ Ok   ✗ Cancel

3. To export the recipes to a file in a different directory (folder) or on a different disk-drive, select the appropriate directory or folder name in the Directories list box.

4. Type a file name for the recipes.

5. Click the Export button.

    The recipes are saved in a new text file with the specified name.

Printing Recipes

Before you print with MasterCook for the first time, you should use the Page Setup command to specify your printing preferences. The Page Setup command lets you specify the size and orientation of the paper you wish to print with, among other options. The Page Setup command in the Windows version of MasterCook also lets you choose the Paper Size and Recipe Design with which to print (functions built into the different Page Views in the Macintosh version of MasterCook).

Make sure that the cookbook's recipe design currently in use is the design you want to use to print your recipes. To change a recipe design in the Windows version of MasterCook, select a design in the Recipe Design drop-down list (or select Page Setup from the File menu). In the Macintosh version, choose a new Design (and Page Layout, if you wish) from one of the Page Views in the cookbook window.

To print a single recipe or a group of recipes (Windows version):

1. Open the recipe that you want to print or select a group of recipes in the cookbook window.

2. Choose Print Selected Recipes from the File menu or click the Print icon-button on the Control Bar.

    The Print Recipe dialog box appears, containing a number of print options.

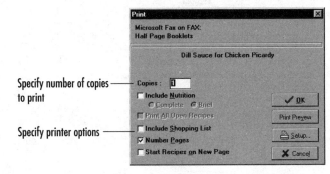

Specify number of copies to print

Specify printer options

3. Choose the options with which to print:

    *   Copies — specify the number of copies to print
    *   Include Nutrition — prints either a complete or brief per-serving nutritional analysis following the recipe
    *   Include Shopping List — prints a shopping list for the recipe
    *   Number Pages — when selected, prints the current page number at the bottom of each page; when not selected, no page numbers are printed
    *   Start Recipes on New Page — prints one recipe per page

Chapter 4

4. Click the Setup button if you wish to choose a new paper size or a different Recipe Design.

    The Page Setup dialog box is displayed.

    To print recipe cards or half-page booklets, choose the appropriate paper size from the Paper Type drop-down list. To choose a different recipe design, choose the new design from the Recipe Template drop-down list. Click OK to close the Page Setup dialog box.

5. To see how your recipes will look when printed before you print them, click Print Preview.

6. When you're ready to print, click the Print button.

    The recipes are printed according to your specifications.

To print a single recipe or group of selected recipes (Macintosh version):

1. In the cookbook window, select the recipe(s) that you want to print.

2. Choose Print Selected Recipes from the File menu or click the Print icon-button on the Control Bar.

    The Print Recipe dialog box appears.

    This dialog box lets you specify the number of copies you wish to print.

3. To print more than one copy of a recipe, type the number of copies you want in the Copies text box.

4. Specify the range of pages to print.

5. Click the Print button.

    A dialog box appears to tell you the recipe(s) are being printed. Press COMMAND-. (COMMAND-Period) to interrupt and cancel printing.

E-Mailing Recipes with the MasterCook Recipe Mailer

Exchanging recipes with friends and family is easy with MasterCook's Recipe Mailer. If you have a direct connection to the Internet — either with an ethernet network or through a dial-up SLIP/PPP link — you can take advantage of this feature to send recipes via electronic mail.

► **NOTE:** The Recipe Mailer requires the appropriate TCP/IP software on your computer. On Windows, make sure that you have the WINSOCK.DLL file. On the Macintosh, make sure both MacTCP and OpenTransport are supported. Unfortunately, the Recipe Mailer cannot take advantage of on-line services such as America Online and Prodigy unless the service provides some sort of TCP/IP connection, such as SLIP or PPP.

To e-mail recipes (Windows):

1. With a cookbook open, select the names of the recipe(s) you wish to e-mail.

2. Choose Mail Recipes from the Recipe menu.

    The Recipe Mailer window appears, containing a list of recipes to be sent.

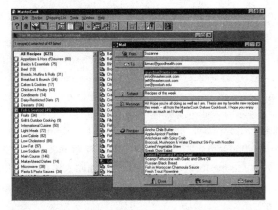

▷ **TIP:** With the Recipe Mailer window already open, you can select additional recipes to send by dragging them from a cookbook window to the list of recipes in the Recipe Mailer window.

Chapter 4

3. If you haven't already done so, click the Setup button.

   The Mail Setup dialog box appears, asking for information about your e-mail configuration. MasterCook needs to know the following before you can use the Recipe Mailer:

   - Your name — enter your full name as you would like it to appear in outgoing e-mail messages.

   - Your e-mail address — a valid Internet e-mail address in the form of *user@host.domain.com*. It is very important that you enter a valid e-mail address, otherwise the recipients of your e-mail won't be able to respond to your messages.

   - Your E-Mail Server's Name (SMTP host) — the domain name of your SMTP mail host, in the form *host.domain.com*, or its IP address, such as *204.118.155.10*. The Recipe Mailer cannot deliver e-mail without this information. Contact your Internet Service Provider or network administrator for assistance, if necessary.

   You need only enter this information the first time you use the Recipe Mailer, or whenever your e-mail configuration changes — MasterCook remembers these settings for the next time you want to send e-mail. Click OK to save these settings.

4. In the From text box, type your name.

   Click on the From button to choose from (and/or create or edit) a list of e-mail names.

5. In the To text box, type the Internet e-mail addresses you want to send the selected recipe(s) to; press RETURN after each address or use commas to separate addresses for multiple recipients.

   Click on the To button to choose from (and/or create or edit) a list of e-mail recipients.

▶ **NOTE:** The To text box requires a valid Internet e-mail address. If the address is formatted incorrectly, the message won't be delivered and you'll probably receive an error message from your mail server. Valid Internet e-mail addresses are in the form of *user@host.domain.com* and contain no spaces or control characters. If you have problems with e-mail addresses, please contact your Internet Service Provider or your network administrator.

---

6. In the Subject text box, type a subject for your message.

7. In the Message text box, type a comment or message to go along with the recipe(s) you're sending.

   Whatever you type in the Message text box appears at the beginning of the e-mail message. You can enter anything you want in this area — introductory notes about the recipes you're sending, or perhaps just a friendly note to the person you're sending them to.

8. Click the Send button to send the e-mail message.

To e-mail recipes (Macintosh):

1. With a cookbook open, select the names of the recipe(s) you wish to e-mail.

2. Choose Mail Recipes from the Recipe menu.

    The Recipe Mailer window appears, containing a list of recipes to be sent.

▷ **TIP:** With the Recipe Mailer window already open, you can select additional recipes to send by dragging them from a cookbook window to the list of recipes in the Recipe Mailer window. (This feature requires Macintosh Drag and Drop, which is a built-in component of System 7.5 and is available separately for earlier systems.)

---

3. If you haven't already done so, click the Setup button.

    The Mail Setup dialog box appears, asking for information about your e-mail configuration. MasterCook needs to know the following before you can use the Recipe Mailer:

    *   Your name — enter your full name as you would like it to appear in outgoing e-mail messages.

    *   Your e-mail address — a valid Internet e-mail address in the form of *user@host.domain.com*. It is very important that you enter a valid e-mail address, otherwise the recipients of your e-mail won't be able to respond to your messages.

    *   SMTP host — the domain name of your SMTP mail host, in the form *host.domain.com*, or its IP address, such as *204.118.155.10*. The Recipe Mailer cannot deliver e-mail without this information. Contact your Internet Service Provider or network administrator for assistance, if necessary.

Chapter 4

You need only enter this information the first time you use the Recipe Mailer, or whenever your e-mail configuration changes — MasterCook remembers these settings for the next time you want to send e-mail.

4.   In the Subject text box, type a subject for your message.

5.   In the To text box, type the Internet e-mail addresses you want to send the selected recipe(s) to. Press RETURN after each address or use commas to separate addresses for multiple recipients.

> **NOTE:** The To text box requires a valid Internet e-mail address. If the address is formatted incorrectly, the message won't be delivered and you'll probably receive an error message from your mail server. Valid Internet e-mail addresses are in the form of *user@host.domain.com* and contain no spaces or control characters. If you have problems with e-mail addresses, please contact your Internet Service Provider or your network administrator.

6.   In the Message text box, type a comment or message to go along with the recipe(s) you're sending.

Whatever you type in the Message text box appears at the beginning of the e-mail message. You can enter anything you want in this area — notes about the recipes you're sending, or perhaps just a friendly note to the person you're sending them to.

7.   Click the Send button to send the e-mail message.

Scaling a Recipe

With the Scale Recipe command, MasterCook lets you adjust the ingredient amounts for a recipe to accommodate a different number of servings than the original recipe. Note, however, that for a variety of reasons related to food chemistry, some recipes simply cannot be reliably scaled. Some culinary experts warn against scaling complex recipes by more than a factor of two and against scaling recipes for baked goods at all.

To scale a recipe:

1.   Make sure that the recipe you want to scale is the current active window.

2.   Choose Scale Recipe from the Recipe menu or click the Scale Recipe icon-button on the Control Bar.

A dialog box appears, asking you to enter a new number of servings.

3.   Type the new serving size and click the OK button (on a Macintosh, the Scale button).

The ingredient amounts are adjusted to accommodate the new number of servings. In addition, the measurement units are also changed where appropriate.

Changing a Recipe's Measurement Units

When it comes to dealing with different measurement systems for recipes, MasterCook offers you unprecedented flexibility. With the Preferences command, you can specify whether you want to use the American (i.e., English) measurement system or the Metric system — or both — and specify up to three decimal places for Metric amounts (see "Setting MasterCook Preferences" in Chapter Seven, "Tools," for more information on choosing a measurement system with the Preferences command).

The Preferences command specifies the measurement system in use when you create a recipe. If you wish to change the measurement system of an existing recipe (or of some of the ingredients in a recipe), you can use the Change Units command on the Recipe menu. Change Units not only lets you change from one measurement system to another, it even lets you change between volume and weight measures for most ingredients. In addition, for any given measure, it displays a list of possible alternative measures from which you can choose the unit of measurement you find most appropriate.

To change a recipe's measurement units:

1.   Open the recipe that you wish to change.

2.   Choose Change Units from the Recipe menu.

A dialog box appears. The Change Units dialog box contains two list boxes: the first is a list of all ingredients in the current recipe; the second is a list of alternative measures corresponding to the selected ingredient in the first list.

Change Units					
Amount	**Unit**	**Ingredient**		**Change To:**	
1	pound	flour		13	ounces
6	ounces	sweet cream butter		109	centiliters
8		eggs		4 5/8	cups
3	pinches	salt		1769 1/8	dashes
15	ounces	ricotta cheese		10 7/8	deciliters
2	ounces	spinach		36 7/8	fluid ounces
109	centiliters	Parmesan cheese		1/4	gallon
1	pinch	black pepper		368 1/2	grams
2	pinches	nutmeg		24 5/8	jiggers
1	quart	heavy cream		3/8	kilogram
4	ounces	mascarpone cheese		1 1/8	liters
2	pinches	white pepper		1089 7/8	milliliters
				3538 1/8	pinches
Change All to American					
Change All to Metric			✓ OK	X Cancel	

3.   To change the measurement unit for a single ingredient, click on the ingredient in the list

Chapter 4

box on the left to select it.

A list of alternative measures appears in the Change To list box on the right.

4. Click on the new measurement unit (in the Change To list box) that you wish to use.

    The amount and measurement unit for the ingredient change in the list box on the left.

    You can continue to change as many ingredients in the recipe as you like by repeating steps 3 and 4.

5. To change all ingredients in the recipe to one measurement system — Metric or American — click either the Change All to American or Change All to Metric button.

    The amounts and measurement units for all the ingredients in the recipe are converted to their nearest equivalent in the corresponding system.

    When you're finished converting measurement units, click the Change Units button to save your changes.

Creating a Nutritional Analysis of a Recipe

You can get a per-serving nutritional analysis of a recipe with the Nutritional Analysis command on the Tools menu. The nutritional analysis includes the total cholesterol, fat, calorie (kcal), carbohydrate, fiber, and nutrient content of the recipe.

To create a nutritional analysis of a recipe:

1. Make sure that the recipe for which you wish to create a nutritional analysis is the current active window, or click on the recipe name in the cookbook window.

2. Choose Nutritional Analysis from the Tools menu or click the Nutritional Analysis icon-button on the Control Bar.

    The Nutrition dialog box appears, showing a nutritional analysis of the recipe.

Nutrition dialog box showing:

Recipe : All Bran Bread

Recipes or Ingredients:	Serves:
All Bran Bread	12

Per Serving Nutritional Information

Calories (kcal):	230.1	% Calories from Fat:	36.3%
Total Fat (g):	9.4	% Calories from Carbo.:	55.8%
Saturated Fat (g):	3.6	% Calories from Protein:	8.0%
Monounsaturated Fat (g):	4.0	% Refuse:	0.8%
Polyunsaturated Fat (g):	1.1	Vitamin C (mg):	2
Cholesterol (mg):	22	Vitamin A (iu):	183
Carbohydrate (g):	32.5	Vitamin B6 (mg):	0.11
Dietary Fiber (g):	1.6	Vitamin B12 (mcg):	0
Protein (g):	4.6	Thiamin/B1 (mg):	0.31
Sodium (mg):	92	Riboflavin/B2 (mg):	0.29
Potassium (mg):	102	Folacin (mcg):	46.0
Calcium (mg):	11	Niacin (mg):	2.9
Iron (mg):	2.3	Caffeine (mg):	0.0
Zinc (mg):	0.8	Alcohol (g):	0.0

Buttons: Print, Done, Daily Values...

3. To view the Daily Values for the recipe, click the Daily Values button.

    Another dialog box appears, showing the nutrient amounts provided by one serving of the recipe, expressed as a percentage of the new FDA/USDA-recommended daily intake of those nutrients (displayed on new food product packaging as "Nutrition Facts").

    Click the Close button (on a Macintosh, the OK button) to return to the Nutrition dialog box.

4. To print a copy of the nutritional analysis, click the Print button.

    The Print dialog box appears.

5. Choose the print options you want — number of copies, font and type size, etc. — and click the Print button.

    The nutritional analysis is sent to your printer.

Chapter 4

6. When you're finished, click Cancel to close the dialog box (click Done on a Macintosh).

▶ **NOTE:** If you use the Nutritional Analysis command with a recipe that uses ingredients not on the Master-Cook Ingredients List, a dialog box will appear, displaying a list of "unknown ingredients" in the recipe but not in the Ingredients List. Click Continue to display a nutritional analysis based on the nutritional information currently available, or Cancel to end the procedure without displaying a nutritional analysis.

Creating a Nutritional Analysis of a Group of Recipes

MasterCook lets you create per-serving nutritional analyses of groups of recipes — so you can create nutritional profiles of entire meals or even an entire day's worth of meals. As with the nutritional analysis of a single recipe, a nutritional analysis of a group of recipes includes the total cholesterol, fat, calorie (kcal), carbohydrate, fiber, and nutrient content of the recipe.

To create a nutritional analysis of a group of recipes:

1. Click on the cookbook window (or Recipe Clipboard window) to make it the current active window.

2. Click on the recipes for which you wish to create a nutritional analysis.

3. Choose Nutritional Analysis from the Tools menu or click the Nutritional Analysis icon-button on the Control Bar.

   The Nutrition dialog box appears, showing a per-serving nutritional analysis for the group of recipes together.

4. To view the Daily Values for the recipes, click the Daily Values button.

   The Daily Values dialog box appears, showing the nutrient amounts provided by one serving of the selected recipes, expressed as a percentage of the FDA/USDA-recommended daily intake of those nutrients (displayed on food product packaging as "Nutrition Facts").

   Click the Close button to return to the Nutrition dialog box (click OK on a Macintosh).

5. To print a copy of the nutritional analysis, click the Print button.

   The Print dialog box appears.

6. Choose the print options you want — number of copies, font and type size, etc. — and click the Print button.

   The nutritional analysis is sent to your printer.

7. When you're finished, click Cancel to close the Nutrition dialog box (click the Done button on a Macintosh).

▷ **TIP:** Using the Nutritional Analysis command with a group of recipes provides you with a handy way to create nutritional profiles of meals or even entire days' worth of food consumption. Because recipes you might group together to form meals may not be grouped categorically — and so are not close to one another in the cookbook window — you may wish to use the Recipe Clipboard as a "storage area" for the recipes, select them in the Recipe Clipboard window, then choose the Nutritional Analysis command or click on the Nutritional Analysis icon-button on the Control Bar.

Saving a Recipe as an Ingredient

Some recipes contain other recipes — for example, a recipe in the *Famous American Chefs* cookbook, "Lamb Spirals with Goat Cheese Ravioli," calls for "Beurre Blanc," a classic white sauce that can be used for other recipes as well. If you had created this recipe, you probably would have wanted to just include "Beurre Blanc" as an ingredient in the "Lamb Spirals" recipe; but if you had done so, the nutritional analysis of the recipe would not have been accurate. To solve this problem, you could simply save the recipe — and all its nutritional information — as an ingredient in the Ingredients List.

To save a recipe as an ingredient:

1. Open the recipe you wish to save as an ingredient.

2. Choose Save as Ingredient from the Recipe menu.

   The recipe and all its nutritional information is saved as an ingredient in the Ingredients List. You can now use it as an ingredient in your recipes. The recipe is saved on disk in the user ingredient file, "User Ingredients."

► **NOTE:** Because MasterCook does not necessarily know the volume amounts of ingredients specified in recipes as whole units (such as eggs, garlic cloves, etc.) or with weight amounts (such as a pound of meat), it does not assign volume amounts to recipes saved as ingredients, but only assigns weight amounts to these new ingredients. If you wish to call for volume measures — teaspoons, cups, etc. — of these recipes saved as ingredients, use the Ingredients List command on the Tools menu to assign volume amounts to them.

Chapter 4

Recipe Cost Analysis

To help you keep track of your food costs, MasterCook includes cost analysis for recipes. However, this cost analysis is based on the individual costs of ingredients, and food costs vary widely depending on a number of factors — seasonality, regional costs, weather, etc. For this reason, ingredients in the MasterCook Ingredients List do not come with costs, although you can add them with the Ingredients List command on the Tools menu. For more information, see "Ingredients and Cost Analysis" in Chapter Six, "Ingredients."

To find the cost of a recipe:

1. Open the recipe for which you want a cost analysis.

2. Choose Cost Analysis from the Tools menu or click the Cost Analysis icon-button on the Control Bar.

   A dialog box appears, containing the name of the recipe, the number it serves, and the cost per serving.

   Click the OK button when you're finished with the cost analysis.

Creating a Cost Analysis of a Group of Recipes

As with nutritional analyses, MasterCook lets you create per-serving cost analyses of groups of recipes — so you can figure costs for entire meals or even an entire day's worth of meals.

To create a cost analysis of a group of recipes:

1. Click on the cookbook window (or Recipe Clipboard window) to make it the current active window.

2. Click on the recipes for which you wish to create a cost analysis.

3. Choose Cost Analysis from the Tools menu or click the Cost Analysis icon-button on the Control Bar.

   The Cost Analysis dialog box appears, showing a per-serving cost for the group of recipes.

4. When you're finished, click OK to close the Cost Analysis dialog box.

▷ **TIP:** When creating a cost analysis for a group of recipes constituting a meal, you may want to use the Recipe Clipboard as a "storage area" for the recipes, because recipes you might group together to form meals may not be grouped categorically — and so are not close to one another in the cookbook window. Then you can just select the recipes in the Recipe Clipboard window and choose the Cost Analysis command or click on the Cost Analysis icon-button on the Control Bar to create your cost analysis for the meal.

5

MENUS & MEAL PLANS

Chapter 5

Managing Menus and Meal Plans

MasterCook's meal-planning capabilities make it easy for you to manage your family's meals, nutrition, and shopping. With menus and meal plans, you can create the perfect combination of foods for a single meal, or plan even the most complex diet for weeks or months at a time. What's more, MasterCook makes it just as easy to create nutritional analyses and shopping lists for menus and meal plans as it does for a single recipe.

MasterCook lets you group recipes and ingredients in two ways: as *single-meal menus* and as *meal plans*. As the name suggests, single-meal menus are for one meal. Meal plans, on the other hand, are calendar-based and may include up to four meals a day for months at a time.

Creating a New Menu

Single-meal menus are especially helpful when you're planning a meal for a special occasion, or when you want to group several recipes together to create a shopping list. (If you want to combine recipes for more than one meal, please see "Creating a New Meal Plan" in the following section.) MasterCook allows you to add recipes (from one or more cookbooks) as well as ingredients to a menu. You can resize both the menu and cookbook or recipe windows so that you can display them side by side; this allows you to drag and drop specific recipes onto a menu.

To create a new single-meal menu (Windows only):

1. Choose New Menu from the File Menu.

   An empty menu appears, labeled "Untitled."

2. Click in the Serves text field and type the number of people you want the menu to serve.

   Recipes are automatically scaled to serve this number of people, up to a maximum of 999. If the number of servings is not specified, the recipes are not scaled (the number of servings specified in each recipe is used).

3. Press TAB or ENTER to move to the first item row and type the name of the first recipe or food item that you want to add to the menu.

   If you're typing a recipe name or ingredient in the new menu window, MasterCook's fast-fill function displays the item most like the one you're typing; if the text you type doesn't match a recipe or food item in the list, MasterCook accepts it as free-form text (but won't provide nutrition or cost analysis information for it).

4. Press TAB or ENTER to accept the highlighted recipe or food item.

   The recipe or food item appears in the menu window. An icon appears to the right of the text you typed, describing the entry type: recipe (recipe card icon), ingredient (measuring cup icon), or text ("T").

Continue adding recipes, food items, and descriptive text in this manner. Press TAB or ENTER after each item.

5.　To add recipes to a menu using drag and drop: in a cookbook window, click on the recipes that you want to add to the menu and drag them onto the menu window.

Repeat this process for as many recipes or ingredients you want to add by dragging and dropping.

To create a new single-meal menu (Macintosh only):

1.　Choose New Menu from the File menu.

An empty menu window appears.

2.　In the About this Menu text box, type a description or introduction for the menu, if you wish.

3.　In the Serves text box, type the number of people that you want the menu to serve.

MasterCook scales all recipes in the menu to serve this number of people. If a number of servings is not specified, recipes are not scaled (the number of servings specified in each recipe is used).

4.　Press the TAB key to move to the first menu item, or click the icon to the right of the icon on the first numbered line.

A drop-down list appears containing four types of menu items:

- Recipe — the name of a recipe in any of the cookbooks that are currently open
- Ingredient — the name of any individual food item; if the food item is found in MasterCook's Ingredients List, it is included in nutritional analyses
- Text — short notes, comments, or descriptions
- New Course — inserts a dividing line into the menu to indicate a new course

5.　Select the type of item you wish to add and press TAB or ENTER.

6.　Type the item you wish to add in the text box.

If you're entering a recipe name or ingredient, MasterCook's fast-fill function displays a drop-down list of available items. When entering individual food items, MasterCook also prompts you for the amount and measure of that food item.

▶ **NOTE:** You can also drag recipes into a menu if your Macintosh System Software supports drag and drop. (Drag and drop is a built-in feature of System 7.5 and newer, but is also available as a separate component for earlier systems.) To add a recipe to a menu using drag and drop, drag a recipe name from the list view of a cookbook window to the numbered-line portion of the menu window.

Chapter 5

7.   Press the TAB or ENTER key to move to the next line and continue adding menu items.

To save a menu:

1.   Choose Save Menu from the File menu (on a Macintosh, choose Save from the File menu or press COMMAND-S).

      A dialog box appears, asking you to name the menu. If necessary, select a new directory (folder) and/or disk drive in which to save the document.

2.   Type a name for your menu in the text box provided and click Save.

      The menu is saved with the name you specify.

Editing a Menu

Once a menu has been saved on disk, you can open it and make changes to it, rename it, print it, or create a shopping list or nutritional analysis for it. As with all other documents in MasterCook, you open a menu with the Open command on the File menu.

To open an existing menu:

1.   Choose Open from the File menu or click the Open icon-button on the Control Bar.

      A dialog box appears with a list of documents in the current folder. If necessary, select the directory (folder) and/or disk that contains the menu that you wish to open.

2.   Select the menu that you wish to open and click the Open button, or double-click the menu's name.

To edit an existing menu:

1.   Open the menu using the Open command on the File menu.

2.   Make your changes to the menu.

      For more information on working in the menu window, see the previous section on creating new menus.

3.   Save your changes by choosing Save Menu from the File menu (on a Macintosh, choose Save from the File menu or press COMMAND-S).

      Once you save the menu, your changes become permanent. If you wish to add or otherwise change a menu but retain the old menu information, use the Save Menu As command on the File menu (Save As on a Macintosh) to save your modified menu as a new menu.

Creating a New Meal Plan

MasterCook's meal plans provide tremendous flexibility. Unlike single-meal menus, meal plans let you plan up to four separate meals a day, so you can plan your family's shopping and nutritional intake weeks — or even months — in advance. Like menus, meal plans in both the Windows and Macintosh versions of MasterCook support drag and drop: you can drag recipes onto specific meals on a specific day on a meal plan, and the recipes will be added to the menu for the selected meal on the selected day.

To create a new meal plan (Windows only):

1.   Choose New Meal Plan from the File Menu.

An empty meal plan calendar window appears for the current month. You can move forward one month by clicking the arrow button in the upper-right of the Calendar window; to move back a month, click the arrow button in the upper-left corner of the Calendar window.

2.   Click on the day in the calendar for which you wish to plan meals.

The day box is highlighted. Click the box in the upper right corner to choose which meal to which you want to add items.

3.   To expand the size of the day box into its own window, double-click on the date in the upper-left corner of the day box.

The day box is expanded into its own window. You can move this day window by dragging its title bar, and close it by clicking its Control menu and choosing Close (or by double-clicking its Control menu).

Chapter 5

4. Click in the Serves text field and type the number of people you want the meal to serve.

    Recipes are automatically scaled to serve this number of people, up to a maximum of 999. If the number of servings is not specified, the recipes are not scaled (the number of servings specified in each recipe is used).

5. Press TAB or ENTER to move to the first item row and type the name of the first recipe or food item that you want to add to the meal.

    If you're typing a recipe name or ingredient in the day window, MasterCook's fast-fill function displays the item most like the one you're typing; if the text you type doesn't match a recipe or food item in the list, MasterCook accepts it as free-form text (but won't provide nutrition or cost analysis information for it).

6. Press TAB or ENTER to accept the highlighted recipe or food item.

    The recipe or food item appears in the day window. An icon appears to the right of the text you typed, describing the entry type: recipe (recipe card icon), ingredient (measuring cup icon), or text ("T").

    Continue adding recipes, food items, and descriptive text to the meal in this manner; press TAB or ENTER after each item.

7. When you're finished, click the meal window's Control menu and choose Close, double-click the meal window's Control menu, or click anywhere on the screen outside the meal window.

    The meal window is closed.

10. Repeat the previous steps to add each day in the meal plan.

> ▶ **NOTE:** You can also drag recipes into a meal plan using drag and drop. Drag a recipe or group of recipes from the recipes list of a cookbook window to the day in the Calendar window onto which you wish to drop the recipe(s). A drop-down list of meals appears; move the pointer over the meal to which you wish to add the recipe(s).

To create a new meal plan (Macintosh Only):

1. Choose New Meal Plan from the File menu.

    An empty meal plan calendar window appears for the current month. Each square in the calendar has four colored bars representing Breakfast, Lunch, Dinner, and a Snack. These colors correspond to the colors in the meal entry area at the bottom of the calendar window (the meal entry area also has sections for Breakfast, Lunch, Dinner, and a Snack).

```
┌══════════ Meal Plan: Untitled Meal Plan ══════════┐
│     [<<]        December 1995        [>>]          │
│   Sun     Mon     Tue     Wed     Thu     Fri     Sat │
│                                           1       2 │
│                                                     │
│    3       4       5       6       7       8       9 │
│                                                     │
│   10      11      12      13      14      15      16 │
│                                                     │
│   17      18      19      20      21      22      23 │
│                                                     │
│   24      25      26      27      28      29      30 │
│                                                     │
│   31                                                │
│                                                     │
├─────────────────────────────────────────────────────┤
│ Breakfast Fri, Oct 6, 1995              Serves  [  ] │
│ [1] T                                               │
│ Lunch                                   Serves  [  ] │
│ [1] T                                               │
│ Dinner                                  Serves  [  ] │
└─────────────────────────────────────────────────────┘
```

2.   Click the day in the calendar that you wish to plan meals for.

The day you select is highlighted, and the display at the bottom of the window changes to reflect the date of the day you're currently editing.

3.   Starting with Breakfast (or whichever meal you wish to plan for), click the icon in the numbered line area at the bottom of the meal plan window.

A drop-down list appears containing four types of menu items:

- Recipe — the name of a recipe in any of the cookbooks that are currently open

- Ingredient — the name of any individual food item; if the food item is found in MasterCook's Ingredients List, it is included in nutritional analyses

- Text — short notes, comments, or descriptions

- New Course — inserts a dividing line into the menu to indicate a new course

5.   Select the type of item you wish to create and press the TAB or ENTER key.

6.   Type the item you wish to add in the text box .

If you're entering a recipe name or ingredient, MasterCook's fast-fill function displays a drop-down list of available items. When entering individual food items, MasterCook also prompts you for the amount and measure of that food item.

7.   Press the TAB or ENTER key to move to the next line and continue adding menu items.

8.   To add items to another meal on the same day, click the icon on the first line of that meal's numbered line area.

As you add items to meals within a given day, MasterCook changes the calendar display so you'll know which meals and which days are already planned for.

Chapter 5

To save the current meal plan:

1. Choose Save Meal Plan from the File menu (on a Macintosh, choose Save from the File menu or press COMMAND-S).

    A dialog box appears, asking you to name the meal plan. If necessary, select a directory (folder) and/or disk to save the document in.

2. Type a name for your meal plan in the text box provided and click the Save button.

Editing a Meal Plan

Once a meal plan has been saved on disk, you can open it and make changes to it, rename it, print it, or create a shopping list or nutritional analysis for it. As with all other documents in MasterCook, you open a meal plan with the Open command on the File menu.

To open an existing meal plan:

1. Choose Open from the File menu or click the Open icon-button on the Control Bar.

    A dialog box appears with a list of documents in the current folder. If necessary, select the directory (folder) and/or disk that contains the meal plan you wish to open.

2. Select the meal plan you wish to open and click the Open button, or double-click the meal plan's name.

To edit an existing meal plan:

1. Open the meal plan using the Open command on the File menu.

2. Make your changes to the meal plan.

    For more information on working in the meal plan window, see the previous section on creating new meal plans.

3. Save your changes by choosing Save Meal Plan from the File menu (on a Macintosh, choose Save from the File menu or press COMMAND-S).

    Once you save the meal plan, your changes become permanent. If you wish to add or otherwise change a meal plan but retain the old information, use the Save Meal Plan As command on the File menu to save your modified meal plan as a new meal plan.

Nutritional Analyses for Menus and Meal Plans

You can create per-serving nutritional analyses of menus and meal plans with the Nutritional Analysis command on the Tools menu. The nutritional analysis includes, among other values, total calories, fat, cholesterol, carbohydrates, and sodium. When you create a nutritional analysis of a meal plan, MasterCook gives you the option of creating a per-serving nutritional profile for a single meal within a day or for the entire day.

To create a nutritional analysis of a menu:

1. With a menu open, choose Nutritional Analysis from the Tools menu or click the Nutritional Analysis icon-button on the Control Bar.

   The Nutrition dialog box appears, showing a list of recipes in the menu and a per-serving nutritional analysis of the menu.

2. To view the menu's Daily Values analysis, click the Daily Values button.

3. To print a copy of the nutritional analysis, click the Print button.

4. When you're finished, click the Done button to close the dialog box.

To create a nutritional analysis of a meal plan:

1. With a meal plan open, select the day (or days on a Macintosh with the Command key, see the Note below) you wish to analyze by clicking the day in the calendar.

   The day you click is highlighted to indicate your selection.

▶ **NOTE:** To select multiple days on the Macintosh, hold down the COMMAND key while clicking on individual days in the calendar. To select the entire month, choose Select All from the Edit menu.

2. Choose Nutritional Analysis from the Tools menu or click the Nutritional Analysis icon-button on the Control Bar.

   The Nutrition dialog box appears, showing a list of recipes in the meal plan and a per-serving analysis of the first day in your selection.

3. To see an analysis of a single meal within the day, click the appropriate radio button for Breakfast, Lunch, Dinner or Snack.

4. To see the Daily Values for the current day or meal, click the Daily Values button.

5. To print a copy of the nutritional analysis, click the Print button.

6. To see an analysis of another day in your meal plan, click the Next Day or Previous Day button to advance forward or back a day in the calendar.

   The day for which the analysis is created is shown at the top of the Nutrition dialog box.

7. When you're finished, click the Cancel button to close the dialog box (the Done button on a Macintosh).

Chapter 5

Shopping Lists for Menus and Meal Plans

Menus and meal plans are a convenient way to plan your meals and keep track of your family's nutritional intake, but with MasterCook's Shopping List feature, you can also plan your shopping weeks ahead of time.

The following section explains how to create shopping lists for menus and meal plans. For more information on working with shopping lists, see Chapter Seven, "Shopping Lists."

To create a shopping list for a menu:

1. With a menu open, choose Make Shopping List from the Shopping List menu, or click the Shopping List icon-button on the Control bar.

    A shopping list window appears with a list of food items from your menu.

2. To save the shopping list, choose Save Shopping List from the File menu (on a Macintosh, choose Save from the File menu or press COMMAND-S).

    A dialog box appears, asking you to name the shopping list. If necessary, select the directory (folder) and/or disk where you wish to save the shopping list.

3. Type a name for your shopping list in the text box provided and click the Save button.

    The shopping list is saved as a document on your disk. For more information about opening, editing, and printing shopping lists, please see Chapter Seven, "Shopping Lists."

To create a shopping list for a meal plan:

1. With a meal plan open, choose Make Shopping List from the Shopping List menu or click the Shopping List icon-button on the Control Bar.

    A dialog box appears asking whether you want a shopping list for the selected day (day(s) on the Macintosh) or the entire meal plan.

2. Click one of the radio buttons to choose whether you want a shopping list for the selected days or for the entire meal plan, and then click the OK button.

    A shopping list window appears with a list of food items from your meal plan.

3. To save the shopping list, choose Save Shopping List from the File menu (on a Macintosh, choose Save from the File menu or press COMMAND-S).

    A dialog box appears asking you to name the shopping list. If necessary, select the directory (folder) and/or disk where you want to save the shopping list.

4. Type a name for your shopping list in the text box and click the Save button.

    The shopping list is saved as a document on your disk. For more information about opening, editing, and printing shopping lists, please see Chapter Seven, "Shopping Lists."

Cost Analysis for Menus and Meal Plans

To help track food costs, MasterCook creates cost analyses for menus and meal plans. However, this cost analysis is based on the individual costs of ingredients, and food costs vary widely depending on a number of factors — seasonality, regional costs, weather, etc. For this reason, ingredients in the MasterCook Ingredients List do not come with predetermined cost values. Before using the Cost Analysis feature, you need to enter costs for the ingredients used in your recipes with the Ingredients List command on the Tools menu. See Chapter 6, "Ingredients," for more information.

To find the cost of a menu:

1. With a menu open, choose Cost Analysis from the Tools menu or click the Cost Analysis icon-button on the Control Bar.

    The cost analysis dialog box appears and displays a list of recipes in your menu along with a total cost per serving.

2. When you're done, click the OK button to close the dialog box.

To find the cost of a meal plan:

1. With a meal plan open, click the day in the calendar for which you wish to create a cost analysis.

    The day you click is highlighted to indicate your selection.

2. Choose Cost Analysis from the Tools menu or click the Cost Analysis icon-button on the Control Bar.

    The cost analysis dialog box appears and displays a list of recipes for that day along with a total cost per serving.

Chapter 5

3.   To see the cost of a particular meal on that day, click one of the radio buttons for break-fast, lunch, dinner, or snack.

     The display changes to show only the recipes for that particular meal along with its cost per serving.

4.   To see the cost of meals for another day, click the Next Day or Previous Day button.

5.   When you're finished, click the OK button to close the dialog box.

6

INGREDIENTS

Chapter 6

About Ingredients

Just as cookbooks and menus are made up of recipes, recipes are made up of ingredients. One of the ways MasterCook makes it easy to type in all your recipes is through the use of the built-in Ingredients List, which includes nutrition, store location, and cost information (which is user defined) for over 5,500 food items. With this list, you can automatically create nutritional and cost analyses of your recipes, and add store locations to shopping lists. You can also add thousands of your own ingredients to the Ingredients List.

This chapter explains MasterCook ingredients: how to find information on specific ingredients; how to add ingredients to the Ingredients List for future use in recipes; how to edit ingredients already on the Ingredients List; and information on adding store location and cost to food items on the Ingredients List.

Ingredients and Nutrition Analysis

MasterCook puts a wealth of nutritional information at your fingertips. With MasterCook, you can prepare a nutritional analysis of a single recipe or an entire menu — or look up the nutritional content of individual food items — automatically, without scanning nutrition tables or doing a lot of complicated recipe math. To provide this instant nutritional analysis, MasterCook relies upon nutrient values of individual ingredients, maintained in the Ingredients List of over 5,500 items that comes with the program (you can add thousands more ingredients to the list, if you wish).

The nutrition information for the Ingredients List comes from United States Department of Agriculture (USDA) research publications. For the purposes of their research, the USDA attempts to use standard (if not always average) quantities in common household measurement units of the most commonly eaten foods prepared in the most typical fashions. For this reason, many of their descriptions of foods can be very lengthy, often too lengthy for the average consumer to want to use in a recipe. We have condensed the USDA food descriptions into usable food item names in average quantities.

▶ **NOTE:** Some recipes in the Cooking Light Digital Cookbook may have nutritional analyses slightly different from those originally printed with the recipe in *Cooking Light* magazine. *Cooking Light* uses even more sophisticated methods of computing nutritional composition than MasterCook does, and their staff nutrition experts take into account many more variables affecting nutritional composition than are currently used by any known computer nutrition analysis program.

Sometimes an item on the Ingredients List describes a foodstuff for which the nutritional information is based on a whole unit, such as an egg, a banana, a fillet of fish, a stick of butter, etc. — as opposed to a standard measurement unit, such as a cup, a tablespoon, a liter, etc. So, for example, if you were to specify a cup of bananas but had chosen the item in the Ingredients List for whole rather than sliced bananas, your nutrition information for the recipe would be slightly inaccurate (because a cup of sliced bananas contains about one and one-quarter whole bananas).

MasterCook helps you avoid this problem by:

- Making the information in the Ingredients List as descriptive of each ingredient as possible, including information about whether the item is in a whole or standard volume measurement unit;
- Displaying in **bold type** the names of all items with nutritional data based on whole units (this is for display in the Ingredients List only; when you add one of these items to a recipe it is in plain text).

So, for example, in the Ingredients List the nutritional data for the item "sliced bananas" is based on one cup of sliced bananas, whereas the nutritional information for the item "**bananas**" is based on one whole banana.

If you ever need to see what criteria MasterCook is using to calculate the nutritional content of an ingredient in a recipe, MasterCook provides easy access to its nutritional information (provided the ingredient is stored in the Ingredients List). Just click on the ingredient name and choose Ingredient Analysis from the Tools menu. A dialog box will be displayed that tells you what weight and volume measurements MasterCook uses to derive nutritional information about the ingredient for the amount called for in the recipe, as well as complete nutrient information on the ingredient for that base amount.

▶ **NOTE:** All food items in the Ingredients List have weight amounts included with their nutritional data, so any ingredient entered in a recipe using a weight-based measurement unit (ounces, pounds, grams, etc.) should provide an accurate nutritional profile.

It's important to note that you don't have to use MasterCook's Ingredients List to specify recipe ingredients. MasterCook allows you to type any ingredient you want in a recipe. (If you wish, you can even tell MasterCook *not* to display the Ingredients List when you're creating recipes; see "Setting MasterCook Preferences," in Chapter Eight, "Tools"). If MasterCook can't find the name of an ingredient in its Ingredients List, it can't provide you with nutritional information on that ingredient.

Chapter 6

This doesn't mean that you have to use the standard Ingredients List names for ingredients if you want to create nutritional analyses of your recipes, however. Besides using the Ingredients List names — in which case you can access the Ingredients List nutritional information — or your own ingredient names (in which case you can't), there is a third way of entering ingredients that combines the two approaches. This third approach is called *creating a link* between an ingredient name and nutritional information for a food item in the list. This technique lets you type the ingredients for a recipe any way you want, then link ingredient names to nutritional information already maintained by MasterCook. For more information on creating links, see "Recipe Ingredients and Nutritional Information" in Chapter Four, "Recipes."

As a final note, it should be pointed out that MasterCook calculates its nutritional analyses based on only that portion of a food which is actually consumed; refuse — bone, shell, or other unused or inedible parts of an ingredient — is factored out of the analysis. This makes your nutritional profiles much more accurate.

Ingredients and Cost Analysis

In addition to nutritional analysis, MasterCook also supports cost analysis, so that you can determine the cost of a recipe or menu. Unfortunately, food costs vary dramatically with geography, seasonality, availability, inflation, and dozens of other variables. For these reasons, we do not include costs for ingredients. You can, however, add costs to the food items in the Ingredients List: using the Ingredients List command on the Tools menu, enter the cost and the amount of the item (1 cup, 1 whole, etc.) on which the cost is based.

For example, to add the cost for flour (based on a five-pound sack of flour) to the Ingredients list, you would first choose the Ingredients List command from the Tools menu, then choose "flour" from the list. Next, you would enter the cost of the flour in the "Cost" box, followed by 5 in the "Per" box, followed by "Pounds". For more information on using the Ingredients List command to add cost information to an ingredient, see "Editing Ingredient Information," later in this chapter.

Store Location

For your convenience, MasterCook lets you track ingredients by the location of items in your grocery store. You can even sort shopping lists by store location, allowing you to group items together by store location. This way, you can tailor your shopping lists to make it easier to find what you're looking for when you shop for groceries.

Each ingredient in the Ingredients List has already been assigned a store location, but you can change this if you like. Using the Ingredients List command on the Tools menu, just select a store location from the pop-up list of store locations, or type your own location name (each new location name you type will be added to the store location list for future use). For information on using the Ingredients List command to add store location information to an ingredient, see "Editing Ingredient Information," later in this chapter.

Finding and Displaying Ingredient Information

MasterCook provides two convenient ways of viewing (and editing) ingredient information: using the Ingredients List command on the Tools menu and using the Ingredient Analysis command within a recipe window.

The Ingredients List command on the Tools menu is the "housekeeping" command you'll use to maintain your Ingredients List. This command lets you find, display, edit, copy, and delete nutritional and other information for any item in the Ingredients List. You can enter or modify an ingredient's weight and volume amounts, store location, cost, and nutritional data. With the exception of calories (kcal), percent refuse, and vitamin A — for which special measurement units have been provided — all nutritional characteristics of an ingredient are given in grams, milligrams, and micrograms. Nutritional information is for the amount of the ingredient specified; this amount may be in either metric or American units.

To find and view ingredient information with the Ingredients List command:

1. Choose the Ingredients List command from the Tools menu.

   The Ingredients List dialog box appears.

2. In the text box above the Ingredients list box, type the first few letters of the name of the ingredient you wish to view.

   As you type, the first ingredient starting with the letters you type appears *fast-filled* in the text box — with the letters you type displayed normally and the remaining letters in the ingredient name highlighted. (As explained in previous chapters, *fast-fill* means MasterCook anticipates the item name you want based on what you type and automatically fills it in for you.)

Chapter 6

3.   Click the Edit button (or double-click the ingredient name in the list).

The name of the ingredient you selected appears in the Ingredient Name text box, and cost, store location, and nutritional information about the item appear on the right side of the dialog box.

When you're done viewing the ingredient information, repeat the process to view another ingredient, or click Cancel to exit the dialog box.

In addition to the Ingredients List command, you can also view and edit ingredient information from within the edit window of a recipe so that you can see information on an ingredient — and change it, if you wish — as you create and edit recipes.

To find and view ingredient information from a recipe window:

■   From within a recipe edit window, click the name of the ingredient you wish to view and choose Ingredient Analysis from the Tools menu.

The Ingredient Analysis dialog box appears, containing complete ingredient information for the selected ingredient. This is particularly useful when you're trying to determine what measurement units an ingredient's nutritional data are based upon, thus helping ensure the accuracy of your nutritional analyses of recipes.

Ingredient Analysis			
Ingredient:	sweet cream butter		
Associated With:			
Amount:	6 ounces	Cost:	$ 0.00
Store Location:	dairy products		
Calories (kcal):	1219.3	% Calories from Fat:	99.5%
Total Fat (g):	138.0	% Calories from Carbo.:	0.0%
Saturated Fat (g):	85.9	% Calories from Protein:	0.5%
Monounsaturated Fat (g):	39.8	% Refuse:	0.0%
Polyunsaturated Fat (g):	5.1	Vitamin C (mg):	0
Cholesterol (mg):	372	Vitamin A (iu):	5202
Carbohydrate (g):	0.1	Vitamin B6 (mg):	0.00
Dietary Fiber (g):	0.0	Vitamin B12 (mcg):	0
Protein (g):	1.5	Thiamin/B1 (mg):	0.00
Sodium (mg):	1406	Riboflavin/B2 (mg):	0.00
Potassium (mg):	44	Folacin (mcg):	4.7
Calcium (mg):	40	Niacin (mg):	0.1
Iron (mg):	0.2	Caffeine (mg):	N/A
Zinc (mg):	0.1	Alcohol (g):	N/A
✓ OK		Edit...	

▷   **TIP:** Not only can you view ingredient information from within a recipe, but you can also change it. To do this, click the Edit button on the Ingredient Analysis dialog box. This, in effect, executes the Ingredients List command and automatically selects the current ingredient for editing; all you have to do is provide the new information. For more information on editing an ingredient with the Ingredients List command, see "Editing Ingredient Information," later in this chapter.

Adding an Ingredient to the Ingredients List

You can add ingredient information for new food items to the Ingredients List with the Ingredients List command on the Tools menu, thereby expanding MasterCook's nutritional and cost analysis capabilities. Once you add ingredient information for a new food item, MasterCook saves that information in a special file on disk, "User Ingredients" ("USER.ING" in DOS), making it available for use with all your future recipes.

Moreover, if you don't like the way we've named an ingredient, you can make a copy of the ingredient and save it with a different name. MasterCook treats the ingredient as a new ingredient. See the next section, "Editing Ingredient Information" in this chapter.

Most commercial foods now provide nutritional information about the product on the package. You can use this information, along with price and store location, to add frequently used commercial food products to the Ingredients List.

▶ **NOTE:** If you don't provide information for a specific nutrient, the value for that nutrient is saved as "N/A" ("not available") rather than "0" (zero), which might lead to inaccurate nutritional analyses.

To add a new ingredient to the Ingredients List:

1. Choose the Ingredients List command from the Tools menu.

    The Ingredients List dialog box appears.

2. Click the New button.

    The insertion point appears in the Ingredient Name text box.

3. Type the name of the food item in the Ingredient Name text box.

4. Press TAB to move to the Weight text box and type the food item's weight as it appears on the package.

    In addition to its name, a weight measure is the only information you *must* supply to MasterCook. Fortunately, almost all product labeling that provides nutritional information provides the amount of the product in a weight measure.

5. Choose the weight unit listed on the product package from the list of weight units to the right of the Weight text box.

    The selected weight unit appears in the box beside the Weight text box.

6. Press TAB to move to the Volume Equiv text box and type the food item's volume amount as it appears on the product package.

Chapter 6

7. Choose the volume measurement unit listed on the product package from the list of volume units to the right of the Volume Equiv text box.

    The selected volume unit appears in the box beside the Volume Equiv text box.

8. Add the cost of the item, if you wish.

    MasterCook lets you specify cost for food items using any size package that you wish. For example, you could enter the cost for an item from a shopping receipt. First, type the cost for the item in the Cost text box; then, in the text box labeled "Per:" type the number of units and choose a measurement unit from the list following this text box.

9. Add the store location and nutritional information (from the product package).

    Press TAB to move from field to field. If you leave a nutrient field blank, the letters "N/ A" appear to indicate that information for that nutrient is "not available."

10. When you're finished adding ingredient information, click the Save button.

    The new food item is saved on disk (in the "User Ingredients" or "USER.ING" file) and appears in the Ingredients List during subsequent uses of MasterCook.

    You can continue in this manner to add information to the Ingredients List for any food items you wish. When you're finished, click the Done button to close the Ingredients List dialog box.

Editing Ingredient Information

The Ingredients List command on the Tools menu lets you change the ingredient information for any item in the Ingredients List. You can also delete ingredients that you don't use from the list, and make copies of ingredients and save them under different names.

To edit an ingredient:

1. Choose the Ingredients List command from the Tools menu.

2. In the text box above the Ingredients list box, type the first few letters of the name of the ingredient that you wish to edit.

As you type, the first ingredient starting with the letters that you type appears fast-filled in the text box.

3. Click the Edit button (or double-click the ingredient name in the list).

    The name of the ingredient you selected appears in the Ingredient Name text box, and amount, store location, cost, and nutritional information about the item appear on the right side of the dialog box.

4. Make any changes you like to the information for the food item — including name, amount, cost, and nutrient data.

    Press TAB to move from field to field. If you delete the information in a nutrient field, the letters "N/A" appear, indicating that information for that nutrient is "not available."

5. Click the Save button to save your changes.

Chapter 6

> **TIP:** To edit an ingredient while working in a recipe window, click anywhere in the ingredient name and choose Ingredient Analysis from the Tools menu; this will display the Ingredient Analysis dialog box. Next, click the Edit button on this dialog box. The Ingredients List dialog box will be displayed, with the current ingredient selected for editing. Follow the instructions above to edit the ingredient information.

To copy/rename an ingredient:

1. Choose the Ingredients List command from the Tools menu.

2. In the text box above the Ingredients list box, type the first few letters of the name of the ingredient that you wish to copy or rename.

    As you type, the first ingredient starting with the letters you type appears fast-filled in the text box.

3. Click the Edit button to display the selected ingredient.

4. Give the food item a new name.

5. If you wish, make any changes you wish to the ingredient's cost, store location, or nutrition information.

6. Click the Save button to save the new ingredient.

    The new food item is saved on disk in the "User Ingredients" ("USER.ING") file and appears in the Ingredients List during subsequent uses of MasterCook.

To remove an ingredient from the Ingredients List:

1. Choose the Ingredients List command from the Tools menu.

2. Select the item you wish to remove from the Ingredients List, either by clicking it with the mouse or by typing the first few characters of the ingredient name in the text box.

    As you type, the first ingredient starting with the letters you type appears fast-filled in the text box.

3. Click the Remove button.

    A dialog box appears, asking you to confirm that you wish to delete the ingredient.

4. Click the Yes button (Remove on the Macintosh) to delete the selected ingredient.

    The ingredient is permanently removed from the Ingredients List.

7
SHOPPING LISTS

Chapter 7

Shopping Lists

With MasterCook, you can automatically create shopping lists for a single recipe, for a group of recipes, for a menu, or for an entire meal plan. This chapter explains how to create, edit, save, and print shopping lists.

Creating a Shopping List for a Single Recipe

To create a shopping list for a single recipe:

1. Open the recipe for which you wish to make a shopping list (or click on the recipe name in the cookbook or Recipe Clipboard window).

2. Choose Make Shopping List from the Shopping List menu or click the Shopping List icon-button on the Control Bar.

   The Shopping List window appears, displaying the food items you'll need to purchase to prepare the recipe, along with the amount of each item that you'll need for the recipe and its store location.

Click on an item's number button to select the entire line

	H	Amount	Unit	Ingredient	Store Location	Recipe/Notes
1		1	cup	carrots	produce	Halibut Orca Bay
2		2	tablespoons	cornstarch	flours	Halibut Orca Bay
3		1	pound	crabmeat	fresh seafood	Halibut Orca Bay
4		1	pint	fumet		Halibut Orca Bay
5		4		green onions	produce	Halibut Orca Bay
6		6	ounces	halibut	fresh seafood	Halibut Orca Bay
7		3	pounds	halibut fillets, split		Halibut Orca Bay
8		2/3	cup	heavy cream	dairy products	Halibut Orca Bay
9		1	teaspoon	lemon juice	produce	Halibut Orca Bay
10				salt and pepper	spices and seasonings	Halibut Orca Bay
11		6	tablespoons	white wine	beer and wine	Halibut Orca Bay
12		1	cup	zucchini	produce	Halibut Orca Bay

3. Click the shopping list window's Close button (or its close box on a Macintosh) when you wish to close the shopping list.

Creating a Shopping List for a Group of Recipes

To create a shopping list for a group of recipes:

1. In the cookbook window or Recipe Clipboard window, select the names of the recipes that you wish to add to the shopping list.

2. Choose Make Shopping List from the Shopping List menu or click the Shopping List icon-button on the Control Bar.

    The Shopping List window appears, displaying the food items that you'll need to purchase to prepare the recipes, along with the amount of each item, store location and the recipes that call for it.

This column contains the recipes that call for each ingredient (some ingredients may be required by several recipes)

3. Click the shopping list window's Close button (its close box on the Macintosh) when you wish to close the shopping list.

▶ **NOTE:** On the Windows version of MasterCook, you can "build" shopping lists recipe by recipe: just drag a recipe name from the cookbook window onto an existing shopping list. The ingredients for that recipe are added to the shopping list.

Chapter 7

Creating a Shopping List for a Menu or Meal Plan

To create a shopping list for a menu or meal plan:

1. Open the menu or meal plan for which you wish to make a shopping list.

2. Choose Make Shopping List from the Shopping List menu or click the Shopping List icon-button on the Control Bar.

    The Shopping List window appears, displaying the food items you'll need to purchase to prepare the recipes in the menu or meal plan, along with the amount of each item (totalled if the item is used in more than one recipe), its store location, and the recipes that use the item.

3. Click the shopping list window's Close button (or its close box on a Macintosh) when you wish to close the shopping list.

Sorting a Shopping List

You can sort shopping lists by ingredient or by store location.

To sort a shopping list alphabetically by ingredient:

■   Choose Sort by Item (on the Macintosh, Sort by Ingredient) from the Shopping List menu.

    The shopping list is rearranged in the alphabetical order of the food items. When you print the shopping list, all items on the list will be printed in alphabetical order.

To sort a shopping list by store location:

■   Choose Sort by Store Location from the Shopping List menu.

    The items on the shopping list are grouped together by store location. When you print the shopping list, the store locations will be printed as headings and their associated food items are printed underneath.

Editing a Shopping List

Editing shopping lists is similar to editing recipes: to change individual items, click in the appropriate text area (or press the TAB or RETURN key to move from column to column), select the text you wish to change, and type the replacement text. To modify entire rows, first click on the number button(s) for the row or rows that you wish to change.

Click on the ingredient row's number button to cut, copy, paste, or clear the entire row

To remove recipe names from a shopping list, choose Remove Recipe Names from the Shopping List menu

	H	Amount	Unit	Ingredient	Store Location	Recipe/Notes
1		3	pounds	halibut fillets, split		Halibut Orca Bay
2		1	pint	fumet		Halibut Orca Bay
3		2	tablespoons	cornstarch	flours	Halibut Orca Bay
4		1	cup	carrots	produce	Halibut Orca Bay
5		1	cup	zucchini	produce	Halibut Orca Bay
6		4		green onions	produce	Halibut Orca Bay
7		1	pound	crabmeat	fresh seafood	Halibut Orca Bay
8		6	ounces	halibut	fresh seafood	Halibut Orca Bay
9		1	teaspoon	lemon juice	produce	Halibut Orca Bay
10				salt and pepper	spices and seasonings	Halibut Orca Bay
11		6	tablespoons	white wine	beer and wine	Halibut Orca Bay
12		2/3	cup	heavy cream	dairy products	Halibut Orca Bay

Basic Shopping List — Close

To add a new item to a shopping list:

1. Click on the item row in the shopping list where you want to place the new item.

    The new item will be inserted in the shopping list in front of the selected item. To append an item to the end of the list, type in the blank row at the end of the list.

2. Choose Insert Blank Row from the Edit menu.

    A blank row is inserted in the shopping list in front of the selected item row.

3. Add information for the new item, pressing TAB or RETURN to move between columns.

To remove items from a shopping list:

1. Click on the number button(s) of the item row(s) that you wish to delete.

    To select a contiguous group of items, hold down the SHIFT key and click on the number buttons of the first and last item row(s) that you wish to select.

2. Choose Clear Row(s) from the Edit menu.

    The item row or rows are removed from the shopping list.

To remove recipe names from a shopping list:

■ Choose Remove Recipe Names from the Shopping List menu.

    All recipe names are deleted from the shopping list.

Chapter 7

To hide shopping list items (Windows only):

1. Click the check box at the front of the shopping list item.

   The item remains on the shopping list but won't be printed when you print the list. This feature is handy when you already have the item in question but may not wish to remove it from the list (for example, if you're creating a shopping list that you wish to save on disk and use repeatedly).

To cut items from the shopping list:

1. Click on the number button(s) of the item row(s) that you wish to cut from the shopping list (and store on the Windows or Macintosh Clipboard).

   To select a contiguous group of items, hold down the SHIFT key and click on the number buttons of the first and last item row(s) that you wish to select. To select a non-contiguous group of items, hold down the CTRL key (COMMAND on the Macintosh) and click on the number button for each row that you wish to select.

2. Choose Cut Row(s) from the Edit menu.

   The item or items are cut from the shopping list and stored on the Clipboard.

To copy shopping list items to the Clipboard:

1. Click on the number button(s) of the item row(s) that you wish to copy.

   To select a contiguous group of items, hold down the SHIFT key and click on the number buttons of the first and last item row(s) that you wish to select. To select a non-contiguous group of items, hold down the CTRL key (COMMAND on the Macintosh) and click on the number button for each row that you wish to select.

2. Choose Copy Row(s) from the Edit menu.

   The selected items are copied to the Clipboard.

To paste items into the shopping list:

1. Click on the place in the shopping list where you wish to paste the Clipboard contents.

    The item or items on the Clipboard will be inserted in the shopping list in front of the selected item.

    To replace an item or group of items with the contents of the Clipboard, select the item row or rows by clicking on their number buttons (so that they appear highlighted); *to insert the contents of the Clipboard in front of an item without replacing it,* click anywhere in the text of the item row.

2. Choose Paste Row(s) from the Edit menu.

    The contents of the Clipboard are inserted into the shopping list.

▶ **NOTE:** If you have copied or cut regular text rather than entire shopping list item rows to the Clipboard, the Edit menu will display the Paste command, not the Paste Row(s) command.

Printing a Shopping List

To print a shopping list:

1. With the shopping list window the active window, choose Print Shopping List from the File menu or click the Print icon-button on the Control Bar.

    On the PC, a dialog box appears indicating the list is being sent to the printer. You can select printer options by choosing either Page Setup or Printer Setup from the File menu. On the Macitosh, the Print dialog box appears.

2. On the Macintosh, choose the print options you want — select the appropriate font and type size — and click the Print button.

    A dialog box appears to let you know the shopping list is being printed. You can interrupt and cancel printing by clicking Cancel (press COMMAND-PERIOD on a Macintosh).

Chapter 7

Saving a Shopping List as a Text File

When you save a shopping list, MasterCook writes it to a text file on disk. Once saved to disk, a shopping list can be conveniently re-opened in MasterCook with the Open command on the File menu; shopping lists can also be edited by any word processor or text editor that reads text files.

To save a shopping list as a text file on disk:

1. Choose Save Shopping List from the File menu (Save from the Macintosh File menu).

    If you've already saved the shopping list, your changes to the list are saved. If the shopping list has not yet been saved as a text file, a dialog box appears, to let you specify where you want to save the shopping list and what you want to name it.

Type name for the shopping list here ⎯

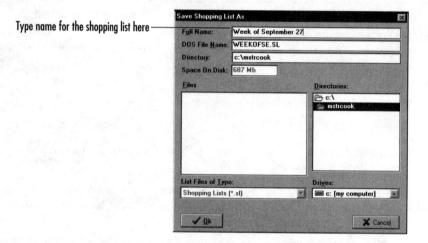

2. To save the shopping list to a different directory (folder) or on a different disk-drive than the one displayed in the dialog box, specify the directory and/or disk-drive where you want to save the shopping list.

3. Type a name for the shopping list in the text box labeled Full Name (on a Macintosh, this text box is labeled Save Shopping List As).

4. Click the Save button.

    The shopping list is saved in a text file with the name specified.

Opening a Shopping List Saved as a Text File

To open a shopping list saved as a text file on disk:

1. Choose Open from the File menu.

    The Open dialog box appears.

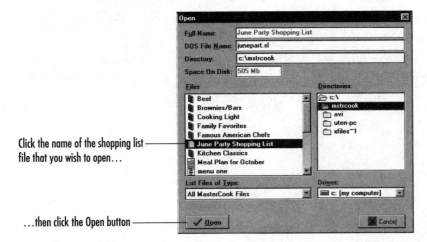

Click the name of the shopping list file that you wish to open...

...then click the Open button

2. Specify the disk-drive and/or directory (folder) containing the shopping list file that you wish to open.

3. Click on the name of the desired shopping list and click the Open button.

    The shopping list text file appears in its own window on your screen.

▶ **NOTE:** Both MasterCook export files and shopping list files are saved as text files so that they may be read by popular word processors and text editors. The MasterCook Open dialog box displays all files that MasterCook can read — including cookbooks, shopping lists, menus, meal plans, and export files.

Chapter 7

Saving a Shopping List with a Different Name

You can save an existing shopping list with a different name or to a different directory (folder) or disk-drive with the Save Shopping List As command.

To save a shopping list with a different name:

1. Choose Save Shopping List As (Save As on a Macintosh) from the File menu.

   A dialog box appears, allowing you to specify where you want to save the shopping list and what you want to name it.

2. To save the shopping list to a different directory (folder) or on a different disk-drive than the one displayed in the dialog box, specify the appropriate directory and/or disk-drive.

3. Type a name for the shopping list in the text box provided for its name.

4. Click the Save button.

   The shopping list is saved with the new name in the specified folder and disk-drive.

The Basic Shopping List

MasterCook lets you create and maintain a shopping list of staple grocery items that you purchase on almost every trip to the store. The items on this list can be added to the shopping lists you create for recipes.

Creating a Basic Shopping List

You don't have to create your Basic Shopping List all at one time, nor do you have to add *all* the items on it to your recipe shopping lists. Add items to the Basic Shopping List as you think of them, and before long it will include all the items you buy on a regular basis. When you don't want to add specific items to a shopping list, you can just temporarily "deselect" those items by clicking in the check box preceding each item that you wish to omit from the shopping list (on a Macintosh, click in the Exclude column of each item).

To create a Basic Shopping List:

1. Choose Edit Basic Shopping List from the Shopping List menu.

    The Basic Shopping List window appears.

2. To add an item to the Basic Shopping List, type the amount and name of each item, pressing TAB or RETURN to move between columns.

3. To mark an item so that it won't be added to shopping lists when you choose the Add Basic Shopping List command, click in the check box preceding that item (on a Macintosh, click in the item's Exclude column).

    A red "X" appears beside the item. To remove this mark and again include this item in shopping lists, click on this "X".

4. Type comments or notes in the "Recipe/Notes" column if you wish.

Chapter 7

5. Continue adding items in this manner; when you're done, choose Save Shopping List from the File menu (Save on a Macintosh).

6. Click the Basic Shopping List's Close button (or close box on a Macintosh) when you wish to close the Basic Shopping List.

Editing the Basic Shopping List

MasterCook provides a number of tools to help you modify your Basic Shopping List. In addition to editing the items on the list, you can also delete items, exclude items, and insert, clear, cut, copy, and paste entire item rows.

To edit items in the Basic Shopping List:

1. Choose Edit Basic Shopping List from the Shopping List menu.

   The Basic Shopping List window appears.

2. Edit the items that you wish to change.

3. Choose Save Shopping List from the File menu (Save on a Macintosh).

To remove items from the Basic Shopping List:

1. With the Basic Shopping List window displayed, click on the number buttons of the item(s) in the list that you wish to remove.

   To select a contiguous group of items, hold down the SHIFT key and click on the number buttons of the first and last item row(s) that you wish to select. To select a non-contiguous group of items, hold down the CTRL key (COMMAND on a Macintosh) and click on the number button for each row that you wish to select.

2. Choose Clear Row(s) from the Edit menu.

   The selected rows are removed from the Basic Shopping List.

To cut items from the Basic Shopping List:

1. Click on the number buttons of the item(s) in the Basic Shopping List that you wish to cut from the shopping list (and put on the Clipboard).

   To select a contiguous group of items, hold down the SHIFT key and click on the number buttons of the first and last item row(s) that you wish to select. To select a non-contiguous group of items, hold down the CTRL key (COMMAND on a Macintosh) and click on the number button for each row that you wish to select.

2. Choose Cut Row(s) from the Edit menu.

The item or items are cut from the shopping list and stored on the Clipboard.

To copy Basic Shopping List items to the Clipboard:

1. Click on the number buttons of the item(s) in the Basic Shopping List that you wish to copy.

    To select a contiguous group of items, hold down the SHIFT key and click on the number buttons of the first and last item row(s) that you wish to select. To select a non-contiguous group of items, hold down the CTRL key (COMMAND on a Macintosh) and click on the number button for each row that you wish to select.

2. Choose Copy Row(s) from the Edit menu.

    The selected items are copied to the Clipboard.

To paste items into the Basic Shopping List:

1. Click on the line where you wish to paste the contents of the Clipboard.

    The item or items on the Clipboard will be inserted in the shopping list in front of the selected item.

    To replace an item or group of items with the contents of the Clipboard, select the item row or rows by clicking on their number buttons (so that they appear highlighted); *to insert the contents of the Clipboard in front of an item without replacing it*, click anywhere in the text of the item row.

2. Choose Paste Row(s) from the Edit menu.

    The items are inserted into the Basic Shopping List.

> ▶ **NOTE:** If you have more than one item on the Basic Shopping List selected when you choose the Paste Row(s) command, MasterCook assumes that you wish to replace all selected lines with the Clipboard contents.

Adding Basic Shopping List Items to a Shopping List

To add the items on the Basic Shopping List to a shopping list:

1. Open the shopping list to which you wish to add Basic Shopping List information.

2. Choose Add Basic Shopping List from the Shopping List menu.

    The items on the Basic Shopping List are appended to the end of the shopping list.

Chapter 7

Excluding Basic Shopping List Items

"Excluding" a basic shopping list item means that, while you wish to keep the item on the Basic Shopping List for future use, you don't *currently* want it added to shopping lists.

For example, you may buy dog food frequently, but not on every trip to the grocery store. By marking "dog food" as excluded, it won't appear on the next shopping list to which you add basic shopping items. When you *do* want to add dog food to your shopping lists, you simply remove the "exclusion mark" in the Basic Shopping List window using the directions below.

To exclude Basic Shopping List items:

■   With the Basic Shopping List window displayed, click in the Exclude box of each item in the list that you wish to exclude.

A red "X" appears in the Exclude box of each item that you click. For Windows users, this box precedes the item; on a Macintosh, this box appears to the right of the item name. The excluded item(s) won't be added to those future shopping lists to which you add Basic Shopping List items.

To include Basic Shopping List items again:

■   With the Basic Shopping List dialog box displayed, click in the Exclude box of those excluded items that you wish to again include on shopping lists.

The red "X" in the Exclude box of each item that you click is removed as you click it. These items will once again be added to those shopping lists to which you add Basic Shopping List items.

Printing the Basic Shopping List

To print a shopping list:

1.   With the Basic Shopping List window displayed, choose Print Shopping List from the File menu or click the Print icon-button on the Control Bar.

On the PC, a dialog box appears indicating the list is being sent to the printer. You can select printer options by choosing either Page Setup or Printer Setup from the File menu. On the Macitosh, the Print dialog box appears.

2.   Choose the print options you want — select the appropriate font and type size — and click Print.

A dialog box appears to inform you that the Basic Shopping List is being printed. You can interrupt and cancel printing by clicking the Cancel button or by pressing COMMAND-PERIOD on a Macintosh.

8

TOOLS

Chapter 8

About the MasterCook Tools

The MasterCook Control Bar and Tools menu offer a variety of special features designed to help make managing recipes faster and easier for you. The Control Bar lets you perform many of the most common MasterCook program tasks by clicking buttons that contain pictures representing the tasks you wish to perform (called *icon-buttons*).

The other MasterCook Tools are commands on the Tools menu. The Wine List command lets you create and maintain a personal wine list. Video Tips allows you to display any videos in your Video Tips directory (on the Macintosh, the Video Tips folder) based on keyword lookups of selected text in recipes, while the Utensils command displays graphics of cooking utensils based on keyword lookups. The Glossary, Seasonings, Substitutions, and Yields & Equivalents commands give you instant access to cooking terminology, measures, and ideas for seasoning foods and substituting ingredients.

The Lookup command performs a "hypertext"-like lookup on selected text in a recipe; when you choose this command MasterCook sifts through all the different reference tools it maintains — from available video tips and the Utensils reference to the Glossary and Substitutions table — and shows you the results of its search. If you wish to use a specific tool to do a lookup — if you wished to see the Glossary entry for a particular word, for example — MasterCook now support lookups for all the reference resources on the Tools menu (including the Ingredients List and the Video Tips, Utensils, Glossary, Seasonings, Substitutions, and Yields & Equivalents commands).

The Preferences command lets you customize the way MasterCook performs certain tasks.

(The remaining commands on the Tools menu are covered elsewhere in this manual: the Nutritional Analysis and Cost Analysis commands apply to recipes and menus and are therefore covered in Chapter Four, "Recipes" and Chapter Five, "Menus and Meal Plans"; the Ingredient Analysis command is covered in Chapter Six, "Ingredients." The Ingredients List command lets you add nutritional information on foods to the Ingredients List that MasterCook uses to derive nutritional analyses of recipes and menus. This command is also covered in Chapter Six, "Ingredients.")

The Control Bar

The Control Bar is the strip of buttons containing pictures, or icons, that appears just below the menu bar when you start MasterCook for the first time. The Control Bar can be hidden if you wish (Hide Control Bar on the Window menu). With the Control Bar, you can perform all the most common MasterCook tasks without ever having to pull down a menu — you just click on the icon-button representing the task you wish to accomplish.

The icon-buttons represent general functions of MasterCook, so that, when activated, they perform different tasks depending on what you're currently doing in the program. For example, if the cookbook window is the active window (the window on top of all other windows) when you click the Print icon-button, the Print Cookbook command is executed. If a recipe window is active, the recipe is printed; if a shopping list window is active, the shopping list is printed.

▷ **TIP:** To see what task an icon-button performs, pass the arrow pointer over the icon-button without clicking on it. The icon-button's function is displayed on the right side of the Control Bar.

Displaying/Hiding the Control Bar

The Control Bar can be hidden (and re-displayed) with the Hide Control Bar/Show Control Bar command on the Window menu.

To hide the Control Bar:

■   Choose Hide Control Bar from the Window menu.

The Control Bar is hidden and the Hide Control Bar command changes to Show Control Bar on the Window menu. To re-display the Control Bar, choose Show Control Bar from the Window menu.

The Wine List Manager

MasterCook lets you keep track of your wines with the Wine List command. This command is useful if you collect wines or if you entertain and like to keep wine information handy.

When you create a wine list, you create one entry for each type of wine for a single year. The type is determined by the wine's maker, type, and year. Thus, you could have two wines from the same maker and year but of a different type (a Riesling and a Cabernet, for example), or you could have two wines from the same maker and of the same type but from different years, such as a 1989 and 1991 Cabernet from the same maker. You could not, however, have two 1991 Cabernet entries for the same maker. Instead, you would record in the Bottles in Stock text box that you have two bottles of the 1991 Cabernet in stock.

Thus, it's important that you enter the producer name, type, and year for each wine you wish to maintain in your wine list. The other fields are optional and are for your convenience.

Chapter 8

To create a wine list:

1. Choose Wine List from the Tools menu.

    The Wine List window appears.

2. To add a wine to the list, click the New button.

    The insertion point appears in the Name text box.

3. Type the name of the wine's producer.

4. Press TAB to move to the Type text box and enter the type of the wine: Bordeaux, Champagne, Zinfandel, etc.

5. Press TAB to move to the Color text box and type the wine's color: red, white, rosé, etc.

6. Press TAB to move to the Year text box and type the year of the wine.

7. Add information to the remaining fields as you see fit:

    • Type the number of bottles you have in stock in the Bottles in Stock text box. You can enter up to 9999 bottles in stock.

    • Type the wine's peak year in the Peak Yr text box.

    • In the Serving Suggestions text box, type any suggestions you have for the way the wine should be served (room temperature, chilled, etc.) or the foods it is best suited to accompany.

8. Click the Save button to save the wine to the wine list.

    The new wine appears on the wine list.

    Continue adding wines in this fashion. On the PC, click the Close button. On the Macintosh, click the Wine List window's close box or choose Close Window from the Window menu when you're done.

Modifying the Wine List

Once you've created your wine list, you can change it whenever you please by choosing the Wine List command again. You can add new wines to the list as well as modify wines already on the list.

To edit the wine list:

1. Open the wine list by choosing Wine List from the Tools menu.

   The Wine List window appears.

Click on the name of the wine in this list, and then click Edit

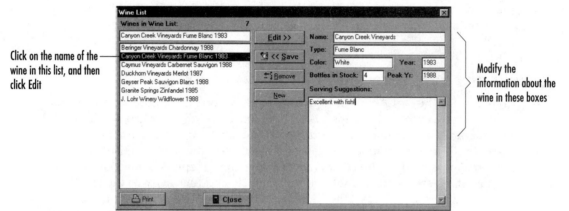

Modify the information about the wine in these boxes

2. To add a new wine to the list, click the New button and type the information about the wine in the text boxes on the right of the window.

3. Click the Save button to save the information about the new wine to the wine list.

4. To edit one of the wines in the list, click the name of the wine you want to edit and then click the Edit button, or double-click the name of the wine you want to edit.

   The information about the wine appears in the text boxes on the right of the window.

5. Make any changes you like to the wine information by modifying the text in the appropriate text boxes.

6. To delete a wine from the wine list, click the name of the wine in the list and then click the Remove button.

   The wine will be permanently removed. Be careful with removing wines from the list with this button — it is one of the few commands in MasterCook that cannot be reversed with the Undo command.

7. Click the Save button to save your changes to the wine list.

   When you're finished editing the wine list: on the PC, click the Close button; on the Macintosh, click the Wine List window's close box.

Chapter 8

Printing the Wine List

When you print your wine list, the number of bottles of each type of wine is printed, followed by the producer's name, the type of wine, and the wine's vintage year and color.

To print the wine list:

1. Open the wine list by choosing Wine List from the Tools menu.

2. Choose the Print button (on the Macintosh, choose the Print Wine List from the File menu, or click on the Print icon-button on the Control Bar).

    A dialog box appears to let you know the list is being printed. On the Macintosh, you can cancel printing at any time by clicking Cancel or by pressing COMMAND-. (COMMAND-PERIOD).

Lookups and Reference Tools

MasterCook features built-in "hypertext"-like lookups for obtaining additional information on words and phrases you select in recipes. For example, you might see the word "braise" in a recipe; unclear of the meaning of the word, you might not fully understand the recipe. With MasterCook's built-in lookup function, you could just select the word "braise" by double-clicking it and choose the Lookup command from the Tools menu. MasterCook would then search through its reference tools until it found a match, and then activate the tool that contained the match — in this case, the Glossary, which would display a definition for "braise." Or you could have simply selected the Glossary tool by choosing it from the Tools menu — it would have automatically located and displayed the selected word "braise."

The MasterCook reference tools supporting automatic lookup include the Video Tips, the Utensils Reference, the Glossary, Seasonings, Substitutions, and Yields & Equivalents. If you select text in a recipe and choose any of these commands from the Tools menu, MasterCook checks to see if the word is a keyword recognizable to the command, and , if so, executes the command by looking up and displaying information on the keyword. If you select text in a recipe and choose the Lookup command from the Tools menu, MasterCook looks through the tools for a match for the text based on the following order of precedence for reference tools:

1. Video Tips
2. Utensils
3. Glossary
4. Substitutions
5. Yields & Equivalents
6. Seasonings

If no match is found for a particular reference tool, MasterCook proceeds to the next tool until a match is found or all tools are searched with no resulting match.

Video Tips

MasterCook will perform "hypertext"-like lookups for video based on any videos placed in the Video Tips list (or, on a Macintosh, placed in the Video Tips folder inside the MasterCook folder). Although no versions of MasterCook currently include Video Tips, the capability exists for you to play video within MasterCook right now. Sierra On-Line plans to publish Video Tip collections for use with MasterCook in the near future; these will include cooking tips from professional chefs, tips for entertaining, etc.

To add videos to the Video Tips list (Windows only):

1. Choose Video Tips from the Tools menu.

2. Click the Add button.

    MasterCook displays a dialog box, allowing you to add videos to the Video Tips list. The dialog box contains a list of video file names next to a list of keywords for the currently selected video.

3. Choose the directory and/or disk drive that contains the videos you with to add to the Video Tips list.

4. Click on the name of the first video to add and click the Add button (or double-click on the name of the video).

5. Type in the keywords you wish to associate with the video.

6. When you've finished adding keywords, click the Done button.

7. Continue this process until you've finished adding videos to your video tips list; then click the Done button.

To add videos to the Video Tips list (Macintosh only):

1. In the Finder, open the MasterCook folder (or the folder containing your copy of MasterCook and its program files).

2. If your MasterCook folder doesn't contain a folder titled "Video Tips," create one.

3. Drag the videos you wish to use into this folder.

    MasterCook will use the name of the video when performing lookups; for example, if you wish to add a video tip on deveining shrimp, name the video file "devein" or "deveining" before adding it to the Video Tips folder.

Using Video Tips

You can use video tips in one of two ways: either select text for which you wish to display video and choose Video Tips from the Tools menu, or choose Video Tips and then choose a video to play.

Chapter 8

To perform a lookup with Video Tips:

1. Select the recipe text for which you wish to play a video.

2. Choose Video Tips from the Tools menu.

    If a match is found for the selected text , the Video Tips window appears, playing the video matched to your text.

    You can use the video controls to play, pause, and stop the video.

3. Click Done when you're finished with the video.

    You can choose a different video to play from the list on the left, if you wish.

The Utensils Reference

MasterCook Deluxe, the Cooking Light Digital Cookbook, and other MasterCook products on CD-ROM include the MasterCook Utensils Reference, an extensive collection of over 300 rendered graphics of utensils, cutlery, and kitchen equipment. You can perform lookups on these cookware graphics as you would any of the other MasterCook lookup commands.

To perform a lookup with Utensils Reference:

1. Select the recipe text for which you wish to display utensil and cookware graphics.

2. Choose Utensils from the Tools menu.

    If a match is found for the selected text , the Utensils window appears, displaying a graphic matched to your text.

3. Click Done when you're finished with the graphic.

    If you wish, you can choose different graphics to view from the list on the left.

The Gallery (Windows Only)

The MasterCook Gallery provides a convenient way to browse through and manage all your MasterCook graphics and video tips.

To use the MasterCook Gallery:

1. Choose Gallery from the Tools menu.

2. Click on the Utensils tab to display the Utensils graphics.

    The Gallery displays six graphics at once.

3. To browse the Utensils graphics, click the arrow buttons in the bottom center of the Gallery window to move forward and back.

4.   To display video tips, click the Video Tips tab.

A single video window appears, along with standard video controls for Start, Pause, Stop, and forward and backward tracking.

5.   To browse video tips, click the arrow buttons in the bottom center of the Gallery window to browse forward and backward.

6.   Click the Close button to close the Gallery window.

Using the Glossary

The MasterCook cooking glossary provides you with instant access to definitions for over 500 of the most commonly used cooking and food terms.

To find a term in the MasterCook glossary:

1.   Choose Glossary from the Tools menu.

The Glossary window appears.

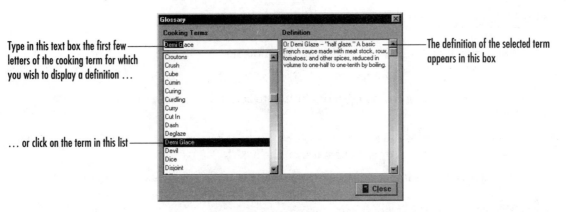

Type in this text box the first few letters of the cooking term for which you wish to display a definition ...

... or click on the term in this list

The definition of the selected term appears in this box

On the left of the Glossary window is a list box containing cooking terms in the Master-Cook glossary; on the right is a text box displaying the definition of the selected term.

2.   Select the term you want defined by typing the first few letters of the term in the text box above the Cooking Terms list (or by clicking its name in the list).

As you type, the list scrolls to display the term in the list that most closely matches the letters you're typing. The term's definition appears in the Definition box to the right.

When you're finished with the Glossary: on the PC, click the Close button; on the Macintosh, click the Wine List window's close box or choose Close Window from the Window menu when you're done.

Chapter 8

Finding the Right Seasoning to Use — the Seasonings Command

The Seasonings command provides suggestions for using spices and herbs in two different ways: you can either view suggestions for a specific seasoning or you can display suggested seasonings for use with a specific food or dish.

Type in this text box the first few letters of the seasoning name...

... or click its name in this list...

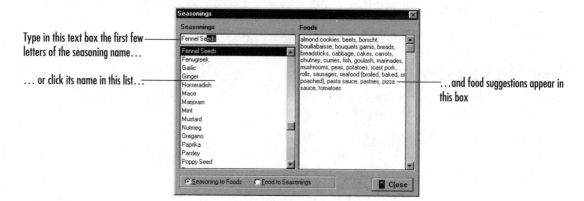

...and food suggestions appear in this box

To find food items for which to use a specific seasoning:

1. Choose the Seasonings command from the Tools menu.

    The Seasonings window appears.

2. Click the "Seasoning to Foods" radio button to select that option (if it's not already selected).

3. In the text box above the Seasonings list box, type the name of the seasoning for which to view suggested foods, or click its name in the list.

    A group of appropriate food suggestions appears in the Foods text box on the right.

To find a seasoning for a food or dish:

1. Choose the Seasonings command from the Tools menu.

    The Seasonings window appears.

2. Click the "Food to Seasonings" radio button.

3. In the text box above the Foods list box, type the name of the dish or foodstuff for which to view suggested seasonings (or click its name in the list).

    A collection of appropriate seasoning suggestions appears in the Seasonings text box on the right.

When you're finished: on the PC, click the Close button; on the Macintosh, click the Wine List window's close box or choose Close Window from the Window menu when you're done.

Finding Ingredient Substitutions with the Substitutions Command

The Substitutions command gives you access to a handy reference of substitutions for a variety of common recipe ingredients. Use these substitutes for ingredients that you or the people you are serving can't eat, or for ingredients that you don't have on hand when preparing a recipe.

▶ **NOTE:** The substitutions provided by MasterCook are at best only approximate substitutes to be used in the preparation of your recipes. The nutritional and caloric values of your recipes may be significantly affected. Taste and texture may also be affected, but less dramatically.

To find a substitute for an ingredient:

1. Choose the Substitutions command from the Tools menu.

    The Substitutions window appears.

Type in this text box the first few letters of the ingredient for which you wish to display a substitution...

... or click on the food item name in this list...

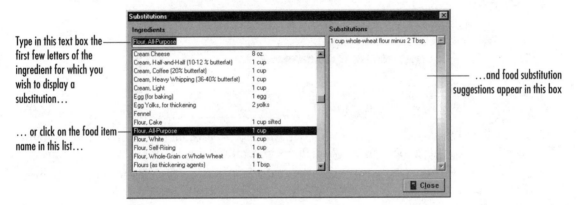

...and food substitution suggestions appear in this box

2. In the text box above the Ingredients list box, type the name of the item for which you need a substitute (or click its name in the list).

    One or more suggested substitutes for the selected item appear in the Substitutions box.

    When you're finished: on the PC, click the Close button; on the Macintosh, click the Wine List window's close box or choose Close Window from the Window menu when you're done.

Chapter 8

Finding Yields and Equivalents

The Yields & Equivalents command provides a handy cross-reference for translating between different measurement units of a given type of food. An *equivalent* is the same physical amount of an ingredient expressed in different measurement units. A *yield* is the amount of a raw item remaining after it has been processed in some fashion; for example, three and one-half pounds of almonds in the shell will yield one pound of shelled almonds.

To find a yield or equivalent for an ingredient:

1. Choose the Yields & Equivalents command from the Tools menu.

    The Yields & Equivalents window appears.

Type in this text box the first few letters of the ingredient name for which you wish to display a yield or equivalent...

... or click on the ingredient name in this list...

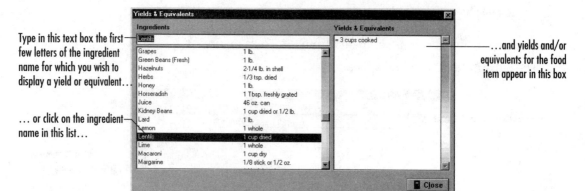

...and yields and/or equivalents for the food item appear in this box

On the left of the Yields & Equivalents window is a list box, labeled Ingredients, containing a list of food and food preparation items in common household measurement units.

On the right is a box, labeled Yields & Equivalents, that provides yields and equivalents for the currently selected ingredient in the Ingredients list on the left.

2. Select the item in the Ingredients list for which you want a yield or equivalent by typing the first few letters of the item name in the text box above the Ingredients list box (or by clicking its name in the list).

    As you type, the list scrolls to display the term in the list that most closely matches the letters you're typing. Yields and/or equivalents for the selected item appear in the Yields & Equivalents box.

    When you're finished: on the PC, click the Close button; on the Macintosh, click the Wine List window's close box or choose Close Window from the Window menu when you're done.

Setting MasterCook Preferences

The Preferences command on the Tools menu lets you custom-configure the way you perform tasks with MasterCook. When you choose the Preferences command, a dialog box appears that lets you specify the measurement system to use in creating recipes as well as options for finding, displaying, and storing recipes on disk.

To Set MasterCook preferences:

1. Choose Preferences from the Tools menu.

    The Preferences dialog box appears.

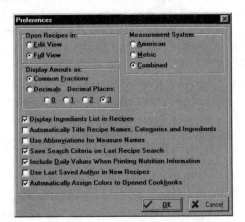

2. Click the radio button to choose whether to open recipes in Page View or Edit View (Windows only).

    The default is Page View.

3. Click the radio button for the Measurement system you wish to use.

    American displays measurement units using the English system — teaspoons, table-spoons, cups, etc. (Americans remain more committed to these measurements than any other people, including the English.) Metric displays Metric units. Combined displays both.

    The default is Combined.

3. Click the appropriate radio button to choose whether to display ingredient amounts as Common Fractions or Decimals.

    The default is Common Fractions.

    If you choose Decimals, click the radio button for the number of decimal places you wish to display.

Chapter 8

4. Click the appropriate check boxes for the following edit and display options:

    - Display Ingredients List in Recipes — When this option is selected (the default setting), the Ingredients List automatically appears when you type ingredients in a recipe window.

    - Automatically Title Recipe Names, Categories, and Ingredients — Capitalizes the first letters of each word in all recipe, category, and ingredient names.

    - Use Abbreviations for Measure Names — When selected, standard abbreviations will be used for all measurement units, in place of the full names. (For example, Tablespoon will be Tbsp, Teaspoon will be Tsp, etc.) This option is by default not selected.

    - Save Search Criteria from Last Recipe Search — When selected (the default setting), the search requirements used in your last search are saved for the next time you wish to use the Search Recipes command. This way complex searches can be used repeatedly with only slight modification from search to search, saving you the trouble of having to continually re-enter your search requirements.

    - Include Daily Values When Printing Nutrition Information (Windows only) — the default is selected.

    - Use Last Saved Author in New Recipes — automatically inserts the name of the last recipe author saved on disk in all new recipes added to the cookbook. The default is unselected.

    - Automatically Assign Colors to Opened Cookbooks (Windows only) — automatically "colorizes" cookbooks when you open more than one.

5. When you're finished setting your preferences, click the OK button to save the preferences for subsequent sessions with MasterCook.

APPENDICES

Appendices

Appendix A: Modifying Page Layouts and Recipe Designs (Macintosh Only)

Once you're comfortable using MasterCook's default layouts and recipe designs, you can edit them to create your own custom designs. Page view has built-in editing features that, when enabled, will allow you to modify nearly every characteristic of how your recipes are displayed and printed.

It's important to remember the distinction between page layouts and recipe designs when editing. (Please see "Page Layouts and Recipe Designs," in Chapter Three, "Cookbooks," for more information.) Because the two are completely independent, you'll edit and save them separately.

Modifying Page Layouts

Page layouts control the physical characteristics of pages — size, orientation, margins, etc. They do not, however, directly modify or control the actual content of the page — that's what recipe designs do. (See the next section, "Modifying Recipe Designs," for more information.) Page layouts are concerned only with how the content is formatted on the page, i.e., the number of columns and/or rows, how much space is between them, and so on. The following are characteristics of page layouts:

- Page height
- Page width
- Margins (top, left, right, and bottom)
- Content areas (number of rows, number of columns, and the spacing between each)

Along with the settings in Page Setup (File menu), these attributes of page layouts give you control over the basic appearance of your pages.

To modify page layout characteristics:

1. With a cookbook open and in page view, choose Modify Page Layout from the Page Layout menu button at the top of the cookbook window.

    The Modify Page Layout dialog box appears with options for modifying the characteristics of the page.

2. In the Height text box, type the height of the page in inches.

3. In the Width text box, type the width of the page in inches.

4. Specify margins by typing in the appropriate text boxes.

    Margins should be typed in decimal notation — for example, "0.5" for one-half inch, or "1.75" for one and three-quarters of an inch.

Appendix A: Page Layouts and Recipe Designs

5. In the Content Areas region of the dialog box, specify the numbers of columns and the amount of space that should appear between them.

    The first text box, Columns, controls the number of columns (vertical content areas) that should appear on the page. To its right is a Spacing text box, which is the number of inches, or a fraction thereof, that should separate the columns horizontally.

6. Specify the number of rows that should appear on the page, plus the amount of space that should separate them vertically.

    The Rows text box is for specifying the number of rows (horizontal content areas) that appear on the page. To its right is a Spacing text box, which is the number of inches, or a fraction thereof, that should separate the rows vertically.

▶ **NOTE:** For most purposes you'll want to design pages with only one or two columns, and only one row. For example, this manual is formatted with one column and one row; most magazines use a two- or three-column format. Too many columns on a page can cause formatting problems, especially on narrow pages or when you use a recipe design that displays ingredients in columns. Use multiple rows when creating specialized page layouts for form-fed index cards or other nonstandard page sizes. Otherwise, one row normally works best.

---

7. When you're done making changes, click the OK button.

    The cookbook is reformatted using the new page layout specifications.

To save your modified page layout:

1. Choose Save Page Layout from the Page Layout drop-down button at the top of the cookbook window.

    The Save dialog appears. Page layouts should be saved in the Layouts folder, which is located inside the MasterCook folder.

2. Type a name for your layout and click the Save button.

    The page layout is saved to disk. You can continue to use the page layout in page view, but it won't appear under the Page Layout menu button until the next time you start MasterCook.

Modifying Recipe Designs

Recipe designs are what you'll edit most often: they control how your recipes look in page view and when printed. Unlike page layouts, which control only the basic formatting of the page itself, recipe designs affect the appearance of the actual content (recipes, in this case) on the page. Each recipe design consists of individual "objects" which correspond to parts of a recipe: title, author, ingredients, directions, and so on. Each object has its own set of attributes and can be modified independently. This means that you have total control over every part of your recipes — you could, for example, create a recipe design that uses a different font for each of the recipe.

Appendices

The recipe design editing features are normally hidden from your view; to edit recipe designs, you must first turn on the layout controls. While in page view, choose Show Layout Controls from the Window menu, or press the CLEAR key. An additional row of icon-buttons — the Layout Control Bar — will appear at the top of the cookbook window.

Editing recipe designs is accomplished by manipulating objects in the cookbook window. When the layout controls are visible, you can click in the cookbook window to select parts of the recipe; MasterCook indicates your selection by drawing a frame around the object you click on. Once you select an object, you can use the tools on the Layout Control Bar to modify its characteristics.

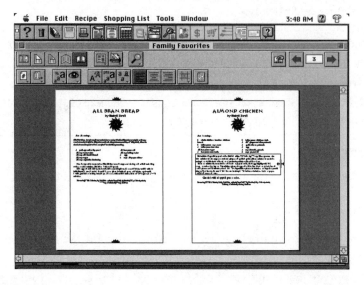

The buttons on the Layout Control Bar are as follows, in order from left to right:
- Page number location — left, right, or center at the top of the page; left, right, or center at the bottom of the page; or none, for no page numbers at all
- Continue next recipe — controls where the next recipe begins: one after another, on next page, on next column, or on next row
- Scale font — scales a font by a percentage of its current size
- Show/hide items — controls whether or not particular parts of the recipe are displayed
- Font — for text objects, controls which font (typeface) is used
- Font size — for text objects, controls the size of fonts
- Font style — bold, underline, italic, outline, shadow, or plain, for no style at all
- Align left
- Align center
- Align right
- Borders — controls borders for the selected object: top, left, right, bottom, or a combination thereof
- Show outlines — draws boxes around each of the objects on screen for easier editing

Appendix A: Page Layouts and Recipe Designs

Most of these buttons require a selection (a part of the recipe with a frame around it) to work; these buttons are dimmed when nothing is selected or when that particular tool doesn't apply to the object you've selected. Other buttons, however, are don't require a selection: the Page Number Location button, for example, and the Hide/Show button. Some buttons also work in different ways depending on whether or not you have a selection: the scale font button, if nothing is selected, scales *all* of the text objects on the screen.

▷ **TIP:** To modify *all* the objects in a recipe design, choose Select All from the Edit menu or press COMMAND-A; any changes you make using the tools on the Layout Control Bar will affect all of the selected objects.

In addition to modifying an object's characteristics with the tools on the Layout Control Bar, you can also control the size and location of objects. Relocate them by dragging them on the page to another location; to adjust an object's size or margins, drag on the edges of its frame.

Using the Page Layout Controls is an experience that rewards experimentation — the best way to create attractive designs is to experiment with the various options. Since your changes aren't saved unless you specifically want to save them, you can always revert to MasterCook's standard recipe designs.

To modify a recipe design:

1. Open a cookbook, and if necessary, switch to page view.

    See Chapter Three, "Cookbooks," for more information on opening cookbooks and using page view.

2. Turn on the Page Layout Controls by choosing Show Layout Controls from the Window menu or by pressing the CLEAR key on your keyboard.

    The Layout Control Bar appears at the top of the cookbook window.

3. Click on the part of the recipe you wish to modify.

    MasterCook draws a frame around the object to indicate your selection.

4. Modify the object by using the tools on the Layout Control Bar.

▷ **TIP:** To make several changes to one object, hold down the SHIFT key while using the tools on the Layout Control Bar; MasterCook won't reformat the page after each change, allowing you to make additional modifications more quickly. The changes you make will take affect the next time you change pages, or when you modify an item without holding down the SHIFT key.

5. Move the object by dragging it on the cookbook window.

6. To change an object's size or margins, drag on the edges of the object's frame.

Appendices

To save your modified recipe design:

1. Choose Save Recipe Design from the Recipe Design menu button.

    A dialog box appears, asking you to name your recipe design. All recipe designs and page layouts should be stored in the Layouts folder, which is located inside the Master-Cook folder, so open the Layouts folder, if necessary.

2, Type a name for your recipe design in the text box.

3. Click the Save button.

    Your recipe design is saved on disk. You can continue to use the design in page view, but it won't appear on the Recipe Design menu button until the next time you start Master-Cook.

Answers to Frequently Asked Questions about Page View

General Questions

What is the purpose of page view? How should I use it?

Page view is MasterCook's way of displaying recipes as if they were printed in a cookbook. Recipes are displayed on pages — on one side of a single page, on both sides, or in book form — and can be modified for appearance with various templates and designs.

Somewhat like Print Preview in a word processor, page view works on the principle of "What You See Is What You Get": recipes are printed exactly as they appear on screen, right down to the margins and page numbers. Use page view for setting up your cookbooks before printing, or to "flip through" MasterCook's electronic cookbooks one page at a time.

Although page view is a convenient way to browse and print cookbooks, you'll want to use list view for most of the things you normally do with recipes, such as creating menus and meal plans, making shopping lists, displaying nutritional analyses, and so on. (Please see Chapter Three, "Cookbooks," for more information on list view.)

What does it mean when MasterCook is "formatting recipes" in page view? How can I avoid the delays associated with reformatting cookbooks?

Changes you make while in page view are applied universally — they affect every page in the cookbook, even the change is something as simple as selecting a different recipe design or using a different font. Frequently these changes affect pagination — a smaller font, for example, might mean that a recipe which used to be on page nine will now appear on page seven, since more text can fit on each page. Regardless of the changes you make, MasterCook always reformats the cookbook *up to* the page you're currently viewing. This can take a long time, especially with large cookbooks or complex recipe designs.

Appendix A: Page Layouts and Recipe Designs

The easiest way to avoid reformatting delays is to make all your changes while viewing the first page in the cookbook. That way, MasterCook has to reformat only one page before displaying your changes.

MasterCook also formats pages when you jump from one place to another within a cookbook — from page one to page forty, for example. Unfortunately, there's no way to avoid this delay, especially the first time you view a cookbook. However, MasterCook does remember pages once they've been formatted, so the cookbook won't be reformatted unless you make changes to the page layout or recipe design, or if you edit the cookbook itself.

Why is there a gray rectangle on the page where a picture should be?

Sometimes there isn't enough memory for MasterCook to display recipe pictures in page view, especially with complex layouts or when more than one recipe is on the screen at the same time.

To alleviate this problem, try increasing MasterCook's memory partition. (While in the Macintosh Finder, select the MasterCook application icon and choose Get Info from the File menu; increase the amount of memory allocated to MasterCook as necessary.) If your computer doesn't have enough memory to increase MasterCook's partition, try closing any unneeded windows and work with only one cookbook at a time.

The text is very small and hard to read in page view. How can I make the print larger?

By default MasterCook displays your cookbook in "fit to window" mode, which means that pages are displayed as large as possible while still fitting completely in the cookbook window. Depending on the size of your monitor and which recipe design/page layout you're using, the text can sometimes be difficult to read.

Zooming the cookbook window (making it as large as possible by clicking the Zoom box at the top right-hand corner of the window) gives MasterCook more room to display pages on screen. You can also select the size at which you wish to view pages by clicking on the Zoom icon-button (the button with a picture of a magnifying glass) at the top of the window: Fit to Window, or any percentage of the page's actual size. Alternatively, hold down the option key while clicking on the page to quickly switch between 100% and Fit to Window.

Why are there blank areas at the bottom of some pages, or why do some two-column pages have text in only one column?

When MasterCook formats the pages of a cookbook, it "fills" the columns and rows much like the way that you read: top to bottom and right to left. Sometimes there isn't enough space to fit large items — pictures, for example — in the space remaining in a column, row, or page. Instead of splitting the item in two, MasterCook carries it over to the available area, which can sometimes leave blank spaces on the page.

Appendices

Empty spaces can also appear between recipes, such as when one recipe ends, but the next recipe doesn't begin until the next page. By clicking on the Continue Next Recipe icon-button on the Layout Control Bar, you can specify when to begin new recipes: one after another, on next page, on next column, or on next row. To minimize the amount of blank space on pages, use the "one after another" option.

Navigation: Finding and Displaying Recipes in Page View

How do I change pages in the cookbook? Can I jump to a particular page without going through the cookbook one page at time?

Use the arrow icon-buttons at the top of the cookbook window to "flip" through the pages of a cookbook, or use the arrow keys on your keyboard. The left arrow key goes to the previous page, while the right arrow key moves forward one page; holding down the COMMAND key while pressing the left or right arrow key will take you to the first or last page in the cook-book, respectively.

You can also type a page number in the text box between the arrow icon-buttons and Master-Cook will immediately switch to that page.

I know the name of a particular recipe in my cookbook, but I don't know what page it's on. How do I find it?

Page view has a table of contents that lists recipe names alphabetically, and, when available, the page number of each recipe. (Page numbers are only available for those recipes and/or pages which MasterCook has already formatted.) To see the table of contents, click the table of contents icon-button at the top right-hand corner of the cookbook window (next to the arrow buttons).

To see a specific recipe, double-click its name in the table of contents. If necessary, Master-Cook will format the pages leading up to the recipe you've chosen. You can always return to the table of contents to "jump" to another page, if you wish. Holding down the COMMAND key while double-clicking on a Table of Contents entry will open the recipe in its own window without reformatting the entire cookbook (up to that recipe) since the recipe is not viewed as a page in the context of a cookbook. It *is*, however, depicted using the current recipe design.

Is it possible to see a recipe in its own window, i.e., independent from the rest of the cookbook? Can I also edit recipes from page view?

Yes. When viewing a recipe in page view, you can double-click on the recipe's title and MasterCook will open a window for that particular recipe. The same recipe design is used as for the rest of the cookbook.

Appendix A: Page Layouts and Recipe Designs

Although you can't edit recipes directly from page view, when you open a recipe into its own window as described above, you can click the Edit button (at the bottom of the new window) to switch to edit mode, which, as the name implies, lets you edit the recipe.

Why are page numbers given for some of the recipes in the table of contents but not others?

MasterCook only knows the page numbers for recipes that have already been formatted. If you've just opened a cookbook that hasn't been viewed before, or if you've recently made changes to the recipe design and/or page layout, chances are that MasterCook will need to reformat the cookbook before page numbers can be displayed.

Once the entire cookbook has been formatted, the table of contents will include page numbers for all recipes, and you can quickly jump to any page in the cookbook without reformatting delays.

Modifying Page Layouts and Recipe Designs

How do I create my own page layouts and recipe designs?

To create a new page layout:

1. Clicking and holding down the page layout menu button, choose the Page Layout that most closely matches the layout you would like to use.

    For example, if you're making 4 x 6 recipe cards, choose a 4 x 6 recipe card layout.
2. Choose Modify Page Layout from the bottom of the Page Layout menu.

    If the Modify Page Layout command is not visible, scroll down the bottom of the menu until it appears.

    The Modify Page Layout command displays a dialog box that lets you change the layout's page size, margins, and number of rows and columns.
3. Choose the appropriate page size, margins, and number of rows and columns and click the OK button.
4. If you wish to add or remove static text or graphics, choose Show Layout Tools from the Window menu and modify these layout items.
5. When you've made your changes, choose Save Page Layout from the Page Layout menu.
6. Type a name for your new layout and click OK.

How do I see the borders of the different parts of a recipe?

MasterCook lets you see the margins maintained by different parts of a recipe, so that you can move and resize parts of a recipe, as well as see where different parts of a recipe start and end with respect to one another.

Appendices

To display the boundaries of the individual items that make up a recipe, choose Show Layout Tools from the Window menu. Next click the Show/Hide Layout Item Borders icon-button on the far left of the Layout Tools Bar; this will display the boundary lines of each part of a recipe, as well as the border maintained by a recipe as a whole (as defined by the current page layout). To turn this border display off, click the Show/Hide Layout Item Borders icon-button again.

How do I put a picture into a recipe while in Page View?

First, use a graphics program to copy your picture to the Macintosh Clipboard. In Master-Cook, open the recipe to which you want to add the picture. If you're in Page View, click the Edit button. Then choose Paste from the Edit menu. The graphic is pasted onto the page and, if necessary, is scaled to fit onto the page.

How do I include my own pictures in page layouts?

When you add a picture or graphic to a page layout, it appears on every page of the cook-book. If you want to add a picture that only appears with a specific recipe, see the previous question or refer to pages 64 and 65 of this manual.

To add pictures or graphics to a page layout, start by using a graphics program to place your picture on the Macintosh Clipboard using the Copy or Cut command. In MasterCook, choose the page layout to which you wish to add the picture. Then Choose Paste from the Edit menu. The picture will be pasted onto the page and will appear in the same position on every page of the cookbook.

How do I move a picture once I place it in a page layout?

First, choose Show Layout Tools from the Windows menu. This will let you click on individual parts of a page layout or recipe design and move, resize, and otherwise modify them. Next, click on the picture and, holding down the mouse button, drag the picture to the place on the page layout where you want the graphic to appear. When you're satisfied with the picture's placement, release the mouse button. The cookbook will be reformatted to accommodate the new picture placement.

Why are some parts of a recipe "split" across page breaks in some recipe designs?

MasterCook lets you choose how you want recipes to "flow" or continue from page to page. You can have MasterCook display and print each recipe at the top of each new page, at the top of each new column or row, or just have the recipes "flow" continuously by displaying and printing each new recipe immediately after the previous recipe.

Appendix A: Page Layouts and Recipe Designs

Some parts of a recipe, such as pictures, are prevented from being "split" across page (or row) boundaries by MasterCook; you wouldn't want the top part of a picture displayed at the bottom of one page and the bottom part of the picture displayed at the top of the next page! Other parts of a recipe, such as directions, are almost always broken up when they cross a page (or row) boundary; otherwise, there would be a great deal of wasted space in your cookbooks.

How do I change the order of recipe items on a page?

To change the order in which parts of a recipe are displayed (and printed) with respect to one another, you'll probably want to display the recipe part borders so that you can see just what you're moving, and where (see the preceding question, "How do I see the borders of the different parts of a recipe?", in this section). To do this, choose Show Layout Tools from the Window menu and then click the Show/Hide Layout Item Borders icon-button on the far left of the Layout Tools Bar.

Next, click on the item that you want to move and, holding down the mouse button, drag it to the place on the page layout where you want it to appear. If the item you're moving is positioned over the *top* half of another recipe part, it will be inserted in the recipe *above* that recipe item; If the item you're moving is positioned over the bottom half of another recipe part, it will be inserted in the recipe *below* that recipe item.

Why doesn't a part of a recipe move when dropped onto an "empty" space?

Because MasterCook displays parts of a recipe only in relation to one another, you must position a recipe item over part of another recipe item in order for it to be moved.

How do I move a picture or graphic from a page layout onto a recipe design?

Pictures on page layouts are drawn on every page; pictures in a recipe design are drawn with every recipe. To move a picture from a page layout onto a recipe design, hold down the COMMAND key, click on the picture, and drag it from the page layout onto the place in the recipe design where you want to display and/or print it.

How do I move a picture or graphic from a recipe design onto a page layout?

Pictures on page layouts are drawn on every page; pictures in a recipe design are drawn with every recipe. To move a picture from a recipe design onto a page layout, click on the picture and drag it from the recipe design onto the place on the page where you want to display and/or print it.

Appendices

Why does the Scale Font icon-button change everything on the page when I have a part of a recipe selected?

The Scale Font icon-button lets you change the font size for an entire recipe by scaling the cookbook's existing text — specified item by item in point sizes — by a factor expressed in percentage. This allows you to make an entire cookbook's text smaller (to allow more text to fit on a printed page, for example) or larger (to make it easier to read on a computer screen, perhaps) with a single command — without ruining the sizes of the parts of a recipe in relation to one another. So, for example, if you want the title of a recipe to remain twice the size of the text in the directions, but wish to reduce the size of the text for the cookbook so that it prints well in half-page booklet format, the Scale Font icon-button would allow you to do this without changing the font size for all recipe items.

How do I change everything for a group of recipe parts or all recipe parts on a page?

Before making changes to a group of recipe items or all items in a recipe, choose Show Layout Tools from the Window menu and then click the Show/Hide Layout Item Borders icon-button on the far left of the Layout Tools Bar. This will display the borders for each item, as well as for the page as a whole.

To make a change to a group of recipe of recipe parts, hold down the SHIFT key and click on each recipe part that you wish to include in the group; then make your changes.

To make a change for all parts of a recipe on a page, choose "Select All" from the "Edit" menu and then make your changes.

How do I control the size of pictures in a recipe design?

First, choose Show Layout Tools from the Window menu. Next, click on the picture that you want to resize; a border appears around the picture. Position the pointer over a border, until it changes to a double-edged arrow. Finally, click on the border and, holding down the mouse button, drag the pointer until the picture is the size you want, and then release the mouse button.

Note that recipe graphics can only be resized by changing the right and left borders. To shrink a picture, move the right and left borders inward. To make the graphic larger, move the borders outward. The top and bottom borders are used to alter the spacing between the recipe graphic and the items preceding and following it, respectively.

Appendix A: Page Layouts and Recipe Designs

Printing with Page View

How do I print on both sides of the paper?

To print recipes on both sides of the paper, you must first click the full-page double-sided view button. Clicking this button will format the contents of your cookbook onto two separate pages. The page on the left side of the window represents the front of the page while the right side represents the back of the page.

Once you have set the cookbook to the double-sided page view, all recipes will be printed on both sides of the paper as depicted in the cookbook window.

Why can't I print the table of contents when I select a range of pages?

The Table of Contents for a cookbook is located before the content pages which contain your recipes. In most books, these pages are not considered part of the content and are therefore numbered with roman numerals. The actual content pages containing your recipes begin at page one.

When you specify a range of pages to be printed, the numbers entered correspond to the desired content pages to be printed.

The Table of Contents can only be printed if you print out the entire cookbook. To print out the entire cookbook, choose Print Cookbook from the File menu but do not specify a range of pages to be printed.

What are half-page booklets?

Half-Page Booklet printing provides a very simple yet powerful way of binding individual sheets of paper into a book or booklet that is half the width of the original paper. For example, using an 11 x 8-$\frac{1}{2}$ inch sheet of paper would result in a booklet that is 5-$\frac{1}{2}$ inches wide by 8-$\frac{1}{2}$ inches tall.

When viewing a half-page booklet in MasterCook, the paper size specified is split in half vertically down the center. The left half of the paper represents the left page of the booklet and the right half corresponds to the right page. Note that the gray line going down the center of the paper denotes the "binding" of the booklet.

How do I construct a half -page book after it's printed?

To "bind" your half-page book pages into a booklet, first arrange the pages with the first page on top and the last page on the bottom. Note that page since each physical piece of paper contains four "half-pages" (two on front and two on back), page one will be located on the front right side and page two will be on the back left side.

Appendices

Once the pages have been put in the order specified above, fold the stack of pages in half keeping page one as the front of the booklet and the last page as the back.

To bind your book, staple down the center fold.

How do I print 3 x 5 and 4 x 6 multi-part cards?

Both 4 x 6 and 3 x 5 recipe cards are available in 8-$\frac{1}{2}$ x 11 sheets containing two and three cards per sheet, respectively. MasterCook provides page layouts that allow you to print your recipes on either one or both sides of these recipe cards.

Printing on only one side of the recipe card sheet is very easy. Simply select single page view for your cookbook with the appropriate page layout (like a 4 x 6 with 2 card per page) and print the desired range of recipes or selection of recipes.

To print on both sides of a recipe card sheet, select double-sided page view mode and the desired recipe card page layout. Note that in normal double-sided printing, the content is first printed onto the front of the page and then continued onto the back.

With recipe card sheets, however, each recipe card must be treated like a miniature page. Because of this, the content must flow from the front to the back of the first card before moving onto the next card. To achieve this effect, you must select "on next row" from the "Start Recipe" menu button. Once set, simply print the desired range.

How do I reinsert pages in the printer to print double-sided pages?

Unfortunately, there is no universal answer to this question because not all printers operate in the same manner.

In general, you must reinsert the pages *in the same order but facing in the opposite direction*. For example, if your printer draws blank sheets of paper from the top of the feed tray, page one must be placed on the top of the stack when printing the backs.

Likewise, if your printer prints on the top side of a clean sheet of paper, you must reinsert the printed pages with the printed side down in order to print the page backs.

Why do I get a different range of pages than I expect when printing a full-page book?

When printing and viewing your cookbook as a full-page book, the goal is to format the contents as it would appear in a real book. Printed books always put odd page numbers on the right hand page and even page number on the left. To put it another way, odd page numbers will always appear on the front of a page while even pages numbers will be on the back side.

Appendix A: Page Layouts and Recipe Designs

If you specify a range of pages to be printed that starts on an *even* page number, MasterCook will print the page preceding it on the front of the page with the requested even page number printed on the back. This assures that the printed page is a faithful reproduction of a full-page book.

When I choose double-sided page view for printing and specify the manual feed tray as the paper source, the page backs are taken from the internal paper tray. What's going on here?

Certain printer drivers do not properly handle the selection of paper trays from one "print job" to the next. There is no good solution to this problem. The only way to reliably do two-sided printing is to always use the "default" paper tray.

Appendices

Appendix B: Exchanging Files Between MasterCook for Windows and MasterCook for Macintosh

One of the many advantages MasterCook offers its users is seamless file compatibility between the Windows and Macintosh versions of MasterCook. MasterCook for Macintosh uses the exact same file format as MasterCook for Windows, so you can literally read the same file on the same disk with both programs. In addition, MasterCook for Windows can read MasterCook for Macintosh export files, and vice versa.

In addition, the common file format used by both MasterCook for Windows and MasterCook for Macintosh is a compressed file format, which means that MasterCook automatically compresses and decompresses cookbook files when saving and opening recipes. Thus, MasterCook recipes take up far less space on disk than those created by competing products.

This section covers the following topics: Reading MasterCook for Windows Cookbook Files with MasterCook for Macintosh; Reading MasterCook for Macintosh Cookbook Files with MasterCook for Windows; and Cookbook File Compression on MasterCook for Macintosh.

Reading MasterCook for Windows Cookbook Files with MasterCook for Macintosh

To directly read MasterCook for Windows cookbook files on MasterCook for Macintosh, you must have a DOS mounter such as Apple's PC Exchange™ installed on your Macintosh. PC Exchange is a control panel that allows a Mac to read disks formatted by a DOS/Windows computer. With MacOS System 7.5 (and later), PC Exchange is part of the system software; earlier versions of Macintosh System 7 can use PC Exchange as well. For information on installing and using PC Exchange, please refer to your Macintosh owner's manual.

Next, you'll want to tell PC Exchange what DOS file extensions MasterCook for Windows uses for both cookbook and export file formats. Unlike the Macintosh, which can recognize file names up to 31 characters long, DOS files can have file names with a maximum of only eight characters, with a three-character extension that indicates the file type. MasterCook for Windows lets users specify cookbook names of up to 80 characters, but uses only the first eight characters of the cookbook name for its DOS file name. On the Macintosh, on the other hand, the cookbook name and its file name are one and the same, so Macintosh cookbook files usually only have names of 31 characters or less. Even if you're using long file names on Windows 95, you'll probably still find it easier to use "eight and three" DOS file names if you're going back and forth between Macintosh and Windows versions of MasterCook.

To maintain complete compatibility with MasterCook for Windows cookbook files, Master-Cook for Macintosh will retain the complete cookbook name — even if it is greater than 31 characters long — for Windows cookbooks that maintain their DOS file names. That is, if you read a Windows cookbook into MasterCook for Macintosh directly — without changing its DOS file name — and don't rename it with the Save Cookbook As command, then Master-Cook will retain its full cookbook name, even if it is longer than 31 characters.

To specify DOS file extensions with PC Exchange:

1. Open the PC Exchange Control Panel.

    The PC Exchange Control Panel window appears, containing a message explaining that the DOS suffix (file extension) assignments listed in its window determine what Macintosh program is used when you open a DOS document from the Finder. This assignment also allows MasterCook to recognize MasterCook for Windows cookbook and export files so that it can display them in the Open Cookbook and Import Recipes dialog boxes. The graphic below shows PC Exchange with the appropriate file exten-sion/document type associations made.

2.. Click the Add button.

    A dialog box appears.

3.. Open the folder containing MasterCook for Macintosh.

    The "MasterCook" program name and small icon appear in the file list.

4. Click on the "MasterCook" program name and small icon.

    The name "MasterCook" and the full-size MasterCook program icon appear in the Application Program dialog box.

5. Type ".MCF" in the DOS Suffix text box.

6. From the Document Type pop-up menu, choose "Ckbk".

This will tell MasterCook for Macintosh that DOS files with this file extension are Master-Cook for Windows cookbook files.

7. Click OK.

A line containing the file extension ".MCF" is added to the PC Exchange Control Panel window, along with information identifying MasterCook as the application program to be used with files bearing this extension.

8. Click Add again.

9. Click on the "MasterCook" program name and small icon; type ".MXP" in the DOS Suffix text box; and, from the Document Type pop-up menu, choose "TEXT".

This will tell MasterCook that DOS files with this file extension are MasterCook for Windows cookbook and recipe export text files.

10. Click OK.

A line containing the file extension ".MXP" is added to the PC Exchange Control Panel window, along with information identifying MasterCook as the application program to be used with files that have this extension.

11. Close the PC Exchange Control Panel.

MasterCook will now recognize DOS cookbook and export files directly, and the Finder will display the appropriate icons for the files.

Appendix B: Exchanging Files

Reading MasterCook for Macintosh Cookbook Files with MasterCook for Windows

Because MasterCook for Macintosh uses the exact same file format as MasterCook for Windows, you can read MasterCook for Macintosh files directly with MasterCook for Windows on a PC. To do so, you must first have PC Exchange or some other DOS mounter installed, so that you can mount DOS-formatted disks.

To prepare MasterCook for Macintosh cookbook files to be read by MasterCook for Windows:

1. Open the MasterCook for Macintosh cookbook file you wish to read with MasterCook for Windows.

2. Choose Save As from the File menu.

3. Rename the file with an eight character name and the file extension ".MCF" and click the Save button.

   While MasterCook for Windows differentiates between cookbook names and DOS file names for its cookbook files, MasterCook for Macintosh does not. For this reason, the MasterCook for Macintosh cookbook file must have a file name that DOS can recognize.

   For example, "RECIPES.MCF" would be a legal DOS file name; "My Favorite Italian Recipes," though a legal name for cookbook files on the Macintosh, would not be recognized by DOS.

   You can, however, retain the cookbook's name even though you must change its file name. To do this, don't use the Save Cookbook As command to save the MasterCook for Macintosh file with a DOS file name, but, rather, just change its file name in the Finder to a legal DOS file name. This way, the cookbook's name will be retained (and will be recognized by MasterCook for Windows) even though its file name has changed.

4. Copy the cookbook file to a PC-formatted disk.

5. In MasterCook for Windows, open the MasterCook for Macintosh cookbook file with the Open Cookbook command.

Cookbook File Compression on MasterCook

MasterCook's file format features on-the-fly compression and decompression of cookbook files. While most users will want to use the automatic file compression, there are some benefits to using uncompressed cookbook files with the Macintosh version of MasterCook that you may wish to keep in mind when choosing to save:

- Recipe searches may be slightly faster on uncompressed files than on compressed files
- If you're running MasterCook for Macintosh with a very minimal memory configuration, you may find you can open more recipe windows with an uncompressed cookbook file than with a compressed cookbook file.

- If you are using on-the-fly file compression software on your Macintosh, you may get better system performance with MasterCook for Macintosh if you save your cookbook files in uncompressed format. This is due to the fact that compressing already compressed files takes longer than compressing uncompressed files.

Compression is applied to recipes on a "Recipe-by-Recipe, Save-by-Save" basis; that is, each time you save a recipe, MasterCook checks to see whether you have specified (with the Preferences command on the Tools menu) that you want recipes saved in compressed or uncompressed format; it then saves the recipe in the appropriate format.

If you are running low on memory and don't have enough memory left to save a recipe in compressed format (the compression program takes up a small amount of additional memory), MasterCook will alert you to the situation with a message box and will save the recipe in uncompressed format.

INDEX

Index

A

adding
> Basic Shopping List items to a shopping list 123
> cookbook categories35
> ingredient to Ingredients List   107-108
> item to shopping list   115
> videos to Video Tips list
>> on Macintosh   131
>> on PC   131

B

Basic Shopping List
> about   121
> adding items to a shopping list 123
> copying to Clipboard   123
> creating121
> cutting items from   122
> editing 122
> excluding items 124
> including items again   124
> pasting items into   123
> printing   124
> removing items from   122

C

CD-ROM
> installing MasterCook
>> Macintosh   16
>> PC 15
changing
> a recipe's measurement units   83-84
> recipe design
>> on Macintosh   64
>> on PC   64
Clipboard
> copying
>> a recipe to   71
>> Basic Shopping List to   123
>> shopping list items to   116
> editing features in recipes   70
> pasting a recipe from   71

Index

Index

Index

F

G

Index

Index

Index

Index

S

Index

Index

V

Video Tips
about 130
Video Tips List
adding videos to
on Macintosh   131
on PC   131
viewing
ingredient information from a recipe window   106
recipes
Edit View   46, 61
Page View   46, 61, 63

W

Web Site
for MasterCook
about   10
web page address   9
for Sierra On-Line
about   10
web page address   9
Window menu
about 20
wine list
creating128
editing 129
printing   130
Wine List Manager
about 127

Y

Yields & Equivalents
about   130, 136
finding for an ingredient   136